GLIMPSES OF

LIFE

BEYOND

DEATH

TONY BUSHBY

Joshua Books

www.joshuabooks.com

Joshua Books
PO Box 5149 Maroochydore BC
Queensland Australia 4558

© Tony Bushby 2004

This book is copyright

All rights reserved. No part of this publication may be reproduced,
wholly or in part, stored in a retrieval system, transmitted or utilized
in any form or by any means, electronic or mechanical, including
photocopying, without the prior written permission of the publisher,
nor be otherwise circulated in any form of binding or cover other than
that in which it is published and without a similar condition being
imposed on the subsequent purchaser. Inquiries for reproduction
rights should be addressed to the publisher.

Master Distribution
Joshua Books

ISBN 0 9751594 1 0

Category: Author: Ancient Mysteries: New Age

Joshua Books

www.joshuabooks.com

ALSO BY TONY BUSHBY

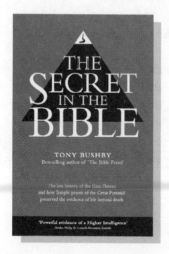 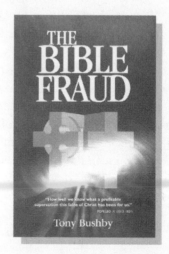

What others have said about Tony Bushby's books...

*I thoroughly enjoyed Tony Bushby's **The Bible Fraud**. Its tale ended my own research into the origins and source material of the Bible (not for a book! Just my own curious hunger to know!). This author has done in a careful and extremely well researched book, far better than most in this genre, because of the attention to detail, which I have confirmed myself over the past twenty years from various sources, is validated and more accurate than many academic papers found in our universities. It is undoubtedly the most important book on Christianity and the Roman legacy ever written, and most likely will have the least impact because it explodes the mythology and power basis for a religion which will be impossible for most to swallow. A truth that will choke rather than enlighten. I look forward to his next book and I do hope that it opens eyes to the true wonders and we finally put away the destructive toy of over simplified pacification tripe that exists in political, commercial establishment religions.*
MAE, Isle of Sanday, Orkney, Scotland

The Bible Fraud*. The ramifications of this evidence are impossible to calculate.*
Rev. Herbert O'Brien, Ordained Minister of the Reformed Baptist Church, Melbourne, Australia

*I have just finished reading **The Secret in the Bible***. *For some reason it doesn't take long to read any of Tony Bushby's work. Perhaps it's the fact that I couldn't put it down once I started reading it! Reading is a passion for me and I must say rarely do I get so much in a book as what Tony Bushby offers to his readers. I eagerly await the publication of his third book. I cannot thank the author Tony Bushby, or Joshua Books for making his books available, enough. Of course the service from Joshua Books was impeccable.*
Edward Sloan, International

*Thank you for devoting so many years to finding out what **The Secret in the Bible** is and for sharing it with others. I'm still in awe over the revelation.*
Charis, International

*I have purchased and read **The Bible Fraud** and **The Secret in the Bible***. *I find the information in them tremendously exciting. They supply missing pieces to the historical puzzle, and lead in a much more realistic direction than traditional explanations. Truth is always better than fantasy, because it is real.*
Whitney Prescott, Stone Mountain, GA, USA

The Bible Fraud *is a real eye opener. It is well documented and easy to understand. Everyone should read this book to understand how we have been deceived. Especially all Christians who think they know the truth. You will never think the same once you have read this book.*
JS, Jacksonville, Florida, USA

*I think that **The Bible Fraud** is a book that has been awaited for a very long time by so many people, and it gives everyone something to think about.*
DG, USA

*Having read both of Tony Bushby's books, **The Bible Fraud** and **The Secret in the Bible** - twice, I wish to congratulate Tony Bushby for writing two such exceptional books and to Joshua Books for publishing them.*
CJJones, New South Wales, Australia

*I recently obtained and read **The Secret in The Bible** and I had to write and say thank you for such a fantastic book. It was not easy purchasing in the UK but the excellent Nexus Bookshop supplied me from here. In this time we live in things are happening at an accelerated rate both in the negative and positive arenas and the truth is a powerful necessity. Both Tony Bushby and Joshua Books have delivered one of the most powerful publications of this age and must both be congratulated by us all. It is a brave step to print such a work when I would imagine that the 'establishment' would rather it remained burried or at least only known by them.*
Danny Grant, London, UK

*I can only say that all heretofore thoughts concerning the NT have been laid to rest since reading **The Bible Fraud**. It brings a perspective to light of "religion" that should be compulsory reading for all honest people. It demonstrates how "religion" was shrewdly used by the ancient rulers much as it is today. The old thought about 'the more things change, the more they stay the same' is markedly demonstrated in this publication. Kudos to the author. Can't wait to read the sequel.*
WB, Independence, MO, USA

The Bible Fraud was ABSOLUTELY FABULOUS.
Tony Bushby has confirmed for me what I have thought to be
true for quite a while.
JAM, Goulburn, NSW, Australia

*After having read your colossal book **The Bible Fraud**, I cannot
find the words to thank you enough for a job well done, not only
did you present the historical truth concerning one of the world's
foremost avatars, but you also gave the locations where one may
find these truths for themselves. It may perhaps be years before
most people will become honest with themselves and open their
eyes to the truth your work has presented to the world, but
thanks to the powers that be, the truth is now an 'open book'. I
personally thank you for a wonderful, fantastic, and noble job
you've done with this work. It has been a long time coming, but
the truth has indeed set us free, and as most people know,
'you can't hide the truth', and most people 'can't handle the
truth'. Thank you again Tony, and I leave you with all good
wishes for peace profound.*
James A McCormick FRC

*On the other hand, a real truth seeker will realise that a guy who
brings his bedroll to a library so he can research night and day
would be an infinitely more reliable source than a writer
whose main focus is fame and ego enhancement.
Congratulations on **The Bible Fraud***
Claudia, USA

*Please send my congratualtions to Tony - whoever he is,
wherever he is - for **The Bible Fraud**. How simple and
straightforward the truth is, when unearthed in such a practical
way. The results of his unstinting investigation will surge across
the world. I hope he keeps his head well down.*
FB, Llandudno, North Wales, UK

*I was truly impressed with the amount of information and references supplied in **The Bible Fraud**. He deserves a lot of credit for his work.*
EP, Toronto, Ontario, Canada

*I am just as fascinated with **The Secret in the Bible** as others. I had delayed my opinion/view because of the 'unknowingly, initiated' process. I felt my mind doing an actual transformation through my entire being. For example: My yearly physical exam surprisingly baffled my doctor. When, she was told I arrived for results, she rushed out, with wide-eyes ... bringing me into an inner-office with colleagues. At first I thought, 'Oh my God, something terrible was found'. Then I had this overwhelming calmness and sat, as the physician opened my records for review. She says, 'Let me congratulate you, Ms English. I wanted my colleagues to meet you. After all of your test results, of all the patients I have examined, I want you to know, not one person around your age (44 years old), is physically perfect of lab tests. Not in 20 to 25 years, have I seen such excellent results! I have told my colleagues that I have not prescribed any medications of any such and you were not on any 'fad' diets'. I tell you this lttle story because I know my physical condition is directly linked to the 'unknowingly, initiated' process of reading **The Secret in the Bible**. I feel like I am on top of the world, mentally and physically. Yes, I have carried the book with me since I received it. I can always find a moment to glance through it over and over and realise there is a 'secret of immortality'. Hey! I am convinced that each individual reader will have their own mind, body and soul revelation when they read this book.*
***The Secret in the Bible** is an 'interactive' guide! My deepest gratitude to you and all the team for making it available.*
Lois, International

Soon from Tony Bushby

THE CRUCIFIXION OF TRUTH

Publication date: 2004

GLIMPSES OF

LIFE

BEYOND

DEATH

CONTENTS

PREFACE

There are few words more rivetting, even awe-inspiring, than 'life beyond death' for they imply, excitingly, that the dead live on to exist in some form of afterlife. Those words have mystery, romance and colour, and according to the historic evidence, millions of people have glimpsed that afterlife in an astounding phenomenon called the Near-Death Experience.

People unexpectedly brought back to life frequently claim to have enjoyed a tantalizing and encouraging, glimpse of the condition to come. Now more than ever before people are returning from the threshold of death and revealing their experiences. Because of modern advances in medical technology, respiration can be restored, hearts restarted, blood pressure sustained and people who would have died in the past are now being brought back to continue their earthly existence.

This book does not provide medical or scientific evidence of life beyond death, but instead allows people who have experienced the afterlife to tell their stories in their own words, and reveal in sincere truth, what personally happened to them. The author gathered many of the experiences recorded in the following pages from personal interviews with over 600 people worldwide who were revived from death, including a 10-year-old girl who drowned in the sea near Brisbane, Australia, and an 83-year-old West Hollywood man who displays his death certificate on his lounge room wall.

Along with a personal death experience recorded in 400 BC, a range of extraordinary new encounters is presented here for the first time. Other experiences are drawn from investigations on the subject done by renowned experts like Dr Raymond Moody and Dr Joel Whitton and together these stories provide a fascinating insight into the state of being suspended between life and death.

CHAPTER 1

A 5000-year-old description of the afterlife

One of the most remarkable accounts of the spirit body and its release when death comes is found in the *Bardo Thödol*, known in English as the *Tibetan Book of the Dead*. It was compiled from the teachings of seers over many centuries in prehistoric Tibet and passed along orally until it was written down around the year 700. But even then, it was sealed with the 'Seven Seals of Silence' for fear that its knowledge would be misunderstood. It has been hailed as 'one of the most remarkable works the West has ever received from the East'... and this is not an overstatement if the book is what it claims to be.

It purports to be a description of the afterlife which is based not upon faith, belief, or tradition, but upon the actual experience of yogis who claim to have died and experienced the conditions of existence after death. They returned through the process of rebirth, maintaining all the while the unbroken continuity of consciousness which enabled them to provide an accurate account of the events that transpired. Thus it constitutes a direct challenge to those who are fond of arguing that no one can speak with authority about death and the conditions that follow it because no one has had any experience of such things.

The *Tibetan Book of the Dead* professes to describe the stage of existence between death and rebirth it calls the *Bardo* state. It was read to the dying person in an effort to help him understand and respond appropriately to what was about to happen to him. It was also read repeatedly after death in a further effort to help the dead person at a time when the teaching is desperately needed and readily applied. These teachings are so detailed and intricately adapted to the apparent changes in the dead person's condition as he progresses through the *Bardo* world, that it is difficult not to seriously ask ourselves whether these wise old yogis and Lamas might not, after all, have pierced the veil which hides the greatest of life's mysteries and caught a glimpse of the existence which lies beyond. And as we look at this document, the striking similarity between the early stages of death, which this book discusses in lengthy detail, and those accounts relayed by people who have come near to death, is nothing short of fantastic.

No true happiness on Earth

The Tibetan *Bardo* is known in the records of other cultures by a host of different names. For example, the ancient Egyptians ... who built themselves meagre houses while constructing the most lavish tombs ... spoke of *amenthe*, where souls dwell in continuous pleasure until descending once more to animate a new body. The Okinawans of the South Pacific spent disembodied existence in *gusho* before returning to this dimension. Australian aborigines believed the soul resided in the earthly haunts of *anjea* between incarnations and observed a ceremony at the birth of each child in order to ascertain from whence if came. The child was later known as having been obtained from a tree, a rock, a pool of water, or some other feature of the landscape, a tradition bearing echoes of Homer's *Odyssey*, which tells how people were 'born of an oak or a rock'. The Hebrews of old envisaged a stay in *pardes* or *paradise,* where eventually they are given instructions for the next life and are sent out, according to the *Zohar*, 'sorrowing in exile; to a place where there is no true happiness'.

The ancients knew what modern man is just beginning to understand ... that the life between lives is our natural home from which we venture forth on arduous journeys of physical embodiment. The ancient Egyptians, for example, made sure their dead were well equipped to face the next world by placing useful objects such as clothing, weapons and cooking utensils as a token gesture of support. In Sumerian society the servants of a household were slain on the death of their master so that they might also serve him in the next life.

Manly P Hall in *Death to Rebirth* compares the experience of incarnation to a diver in a diving suit leaving the light and fresh air in which he is comfortable and descending, by lifeline, to the bottom of the sea ...

> ... the heavy diving suit is the physical body and the sea the ocean of life. At birth the man assumes the diving suit, but his spirit is always connected by a line to the light above. Man descends into the depths of the sea of sorrow and mortality that he may find there the hidden treasure of wisdom, for experience and understanding are pearls of great price and to gain them man must bear all things. When the treasure has been found, or his hours of labour

are over, he is drawn back into the boat again, and taking off the heavy armour breathes the fresh air and feels free once more. Wise men realize that this incident we call life is only one trip to the bottom of the sea; that we have been down many times before and must go down many times again before we find the treasure.

Scriptural and mythological writing relate other common features of the between-life state, among them a sense of timelessness, the rapturous intrusion of an overwhelmingly bright light, a panoramic review of the life just passed and the soul's judgment, which is usually attended by three wise figures.

CHAPTER 2

The joy of death is concealed so that we may endure life

It is now 20 years since Dr Raymond Moody's first book, *Life After Life*, the first survey of the Near-Death Experience (NDE), became a bestseller and these passages relay his reconstruction of a complete 'dying' experience combining all the elements that were describe to him.

A man is dying and, as he reaches the point of greatest physical distress, he hears himself pronounced dead by his doctor. He begins to hear an uncomfortable noise, a loud ringing or buzzing, and at the same time feels himself moving very rapidly through a long dark tunnel.

After this he suddenly finds himself outside of his own physical body, but still in the immediate physical environment, and he watches his own body from a distance, as though he is a spectator. He watches the resuscitating attempt from this unusual vantage point and in a state of emotional upheaval. After a while, he collects himself and becomes more accustomed to his odd condition. He notices that he still has a 'body', but one of a very different nature and with very different powers from the physical body he has left behind.

Soon other things begin to happen. Others come to meet and help him. He glimpses the spirits of relatives and friends who have already died, and a loving, warm spirit of a kind he has never encountered before ... a Being of light ... appears before him. This Being asks him a question, non-verbally, to make him evaluate his life and helps him along by showing him a panoramic, instantaneous playback of the major events of his life.

At some point he finds himself approaching some sort of barrier or border, apparently representing the limit between earthly life and the next. Yet, he finds that he must go back to the Earth, as the time for his death has not yet come. At this point he resists, for now he is taken up with his experiences in the afterlife and does not want to return. He is overwhelmed by intense feelings of joy, love and peace. Despite his attitude though, he somehow reunites with his physical body and lives.

Later he tries to tell others, but he has trouble doing so. In the first place, he can find no human words adequate to describe these unearthly episodes. He also finds that others scoff, so he stops telling other people. Still, the experience affects his life profoundly, especially his views about death and its relationship to life.

This is an accurate description of the NDE at, and soon after, the moment of death and was compiled by Dr Moody after his systematic study of 2000 people who were revived from clinical death.

What happens to us when we die?

It is fascinating to contemplate near-death incidents and to speculate about what the afterlife may be like. Because of the fascinating nature of the topic, George Gallup Jnr decided several years ago to turn the full resources of the Gallup Poll towards an explanation of the afterlife. A special focus in this study was the involvement of Americans in 'near-death' or 'verge-of-death' experiences. This poll represented the most comprehensive national survey about the experience with the near-death and afterlife encounters that had ever been undertaken.

George Gallop's studies found that approximately 23 million people have had a verge-of-death or near-death experience and of that number about 8 million have experienced some sort of mystical encounter along with the death event. After a death crisis occurs, many people find themselves catapulted into another dimension of reality. It is clear that something out of the ordinary occurs and an adventure begins.

What is clinical death?

Clinical death is described as the state during which all external signs of life, the medically detectable signs of reflexes, consciousness, respiration and cardiac activity, are absent. A clinically dead person has no heartbeat or pulse, breathing stops for an extended period, blood pressure drops so low as to be undetectable, the pupils of the eyes dilate totally, the lips and skin begin to discolour and the body temperature drops and continues to decrease. The medical fraternity has used these criteria for years and it is during this period that people claim to have existed in a manner other than their physical body, and talk of a continuation of conscious experience.

CHAPTER 3

Return from the brink of tranquillity

Professor Kenneth Ring of the University of Connecticut, described a widely accepted sequence of stages in the NDE. The first stage is characterized by an overwhelming sense of peace, calm, and well being, as well as freedom from any body pain. In the second stage the Experiencer feels detached from the physical body, which is often seen below and in a slightly different light. The detachment is emotional as well as physical; the self no longer identifies with what it sees as a physical instrument to be discarded when worn out. There is a sensation of weightlessness, mental processes are very clear and the senses of sight and hearing extremely acute.

Hearing seems to be telepathic ... 'I heard him say, or rather, saw him think'. Experiencers are often able to describe in detail events that took place while they were 'unconscious'. Evidence like this lends weight to a partially objective interpretation of the experience, against the contention that it is simply a wish-fulfilling delusion or hallucination. One test, in fact, concluded that people asked to fabricate resuscitation, make serious errors. Sometimes these two stages are bypassed and the Experiencers find themselves moving rapidly down a dark tunnel towards a light. Some researchers interpret this third stage as a transition into another mode of consciousness.

In stage four, the light gradually expands until the Experiencer merges into it. There's a feeling of love, joy, beauty, and peace; the light exudes compassion and understanding and may be felt as a presence or a being with whom the Experiencer feels at one, which some call an encounter with the 'Higher Self'.

At this point, the Experiencer may have the impression of seeing their earthly life in review, discovering that nothing has been erased; not only life experiences, but also the effects of thoughts, feelings and actions on others are now felt as if they (the Experiencer) were at the receiving end. The moral implications of this are momentous, implying that we are so linked to each other that we undergo the reverberations of all we think, say, feel or do. For the Experiencer, awareness and control of thoughts, feelings and actions become a central concern.

The final and deepest stage is 'entering the light', into a transcendental environment of unsurpassed beauty. There may be meetings with dead relatives and loved ones, who usually make it clear that the Experiencer's time is not yet up and they must return to Earth.

Sometimes the return is symbolically presaged by a door, boundary or river which they are not allowed to cross. People return for two main reasons: either their purpose has not been fulfilled or they must meet the needs of family and dependants.

Many at first are distressed and disappointed to find themselves back in the physical body with its pain and limitations. 'Death is the hardest thing from the outside and as long as we are outside of it', wrote CG Jung, after his own NDE in 1944. 'But once inside, you taste of such completeness and peace and fulfillment that you don't want to return'.

He found his illness gave him a glimpse behind the veil into what he called the truly real life; he was horrified at the prospect of returning to 'this fragmentary, restricted, narrow, almost mechanical life, where you were subject to the laws of gravity and cohesion, imprisoned in a system of three dimensions and whirled along with other bodies in the turbulent stream of time'.

For Jung, death, far from being the irreversible extinction of consciousness, heralded an expansion and intensification of experience. It was our physical reality which now seemed unreal, limited and robot-like; a complete revolution of perspective and assumptions.

CHAPTER 4

Intriguing near-death and beyond-life experiences

After 25 years of research and investigation into these matters there is now plenty of evidence to support the existence of life beyond death and the following stories are typical of the NDE.

One elderly woman with a heart condition relayed her story: 'I had pains in the chest and lay on the davenport and felt like I was fainting. During this time, my deceased mother came and stood beside me and said, 'Gail, come with me'. 'As she started to walk away, I tried to get up to follow her. But I fell on the floor in a great deal of pain. She continued to walk away and walked *through* the dining room table and the wall and then disappeared. I feel that if she had not been there I would have lost my life'.

In another incident, a Californian social worker said he was suffering from a strep throat infection for which no antibiotics were immediately available. He was treated with heat packs, which were supposed to limit the infection, and was finally taken to hospital for more extensive treatment. While waiting for medical assistance, he 'had the sensation of floating two or three feet above the table. There were no lights, personages, etc. I felt like I had unfinished business on Earth. I awoke days later, alive, after having undergone a tracheotomy'.

A university student from Wisconsin said, 'I had surgery and when I was in the recovery room, I stopped breathing. As they worked on me, I remember feeling like I was not in my body. But I could hear them talking and I felt that I was floating. It was very black where I was ... and I was at peace. God said in a loud thundering voice, 'Go back ... you work is not yet done'... Spirits then pushed me back'.

More dramatic, graphic images came to a 50-year-old factory worker from Illinois. After his appendix burst, he was rushed into hospital where doctors pronounced him dead. They left him on the operating table, during which time, he reported, 'I saw my (dead) mother. She was in the most beautiful place ... a real bright light ... flowers and streams. She told me she was very happy. But she also told me I was to go back home, many people needed me ... everything would work out ... that she wasn't ready for me yet. She said that they (my family) needed me back home. She then bid me goodbye at a white bridge spanning a golden stream. I started walking slowly back. Then I came to, and the nurses and doctors said that I had died for a time'.

In another situation, a Texas man, by his own report, was 'close to death' and was 'ushered into a strikingly beautiful palace'. He said, 'I heard a voice tell me to spread the word about how beautiful that place was'. It was a beautiful place ... flowers, trees of all kinds, beautiful gardens ... tremendous happiness filled me. The voice said, 'It is the house of David'.

In one account given, a strange presence appeared to a grandmother who was sleeping near her grandchild. This woman often spent hours at night in prayer, and so she was quite sensitive to the spiritual realm. As she was sleeping that night, she was aroused suddenly by something, and when she looked up, she saw a strange creature 'bound up in light but with a human form'. The being, which she identified as an angel, said nothing, but pointed urgently toward the room where the woman's grandchild was sleeping in a crib. 'I sensed I had to get up immediately and go into my grandson's room', she recalled.

When she looked into the baby's crib, she confronted a horrifying sight. 'The baby had been given a glass milk bottle during the night but had cracked it, and a blade of glass, like a knife, was resting precariously against the child's throat'.

This woman believed fervently that her grandchild's life was saved 'by an angelic intervention. If he had moved, that would have been it. I think that it was his guardian angel that warned me'.

Terry Smith of Lima, Pa is living proof that there is life beyond death ... she died and came back to talk about it. Terry, 35, had just returned from a wedding with her boyfriend, Jim, when she had an allergic reaction to something she ate. She said Jim realized that they didn't have time to wait for an ambulance and he rushed her to hospital. 'My throat closed up and suffocated me. I was blue from the belly button up, and had no pulse', said Terry, after paramedics worked to revive her.

Terry was dead for a few minutes and described it as a wonderful experience that changed her life for the better. 'I was kind of floating over the Earth ... I had no weight and I was transparent. It was very peaceful and I wasn't afraid at all. I could see a bright light at the end of a tunnel and a superior being in the form of a male voice asked me, 'Are you ready?'... and I said, 'NO!' Terry woke up in the hospital two days later. She was hooked to life-support machines and spent another two days in intensive care. 'The experience has given me a lot more confidence; I feel so good to be here. I've made a will and everything in my house is clean and ready if I were to die tomorrow. When my time comes I'll be ready', she said.

Margaret Heineman is living for the day she dies ... for the second time. The 68-year-old grandmother of five was with her husband Harry when they were involved in a head-on motor vehicle accident outside of Bern in Switzerland. Harry died instantly of a broken neck and head injuries. Just as the ambulance arrived at the hospital Margaret died too, but doctors managed to revive her. To this day the former schoolteacher can remember the moment of her death and her hand-in-hand trip into Heaven with her husband Harry. 'We were happy there together, but it only lasted for a few minutes', she said in an article for her church paper, the *Lutheran Church Bulletin*. 'The next thing I remember is waking up in the emergency room racked by pain. Now I have to live my last days without Harry. We were married for 51 years. The doctors told me that I was brought in without a pulse and with internal injuries. They said it took them about three minutes to get my pulse back and stop the haemorrhaging.'

'I don't remember any of that. But what I do remember is like a beautiful vision. I was lying on the stretcher and I saw Harry coming to me. The next thing I knew I was floating above my body, holding hands with my husband. The two of us walked towards a brilliant white light and the warmest, sweetest, feelings enveloped us. We came to a beautiful place where our dead son, Anders, waited for us. We were just so happy to all be together'. She remembers her return to life as a shock and disappointment, but believes it was God's will. 'That's the only thing that's keeping me going without Harry', she said. 'I pray that I can serve Him in the way He wants and that He will soon let me return to Heaven to be with Harry'.

'What I saw in Heaven'

This is the story of Mrs Nyks of Brisbane, Australia, who had a near-death experience in Germany in 1984. 'I got very ill at home. I had a feeling that something wanted to leave my body as I collapsed. I felt like I was nearly dead and had a feeling of the doctor being around me. Suddenly, I left my body as a soul and travelled very quickly through a tunnel into an immense bright light. I was able to see a lot of pictures before me on a big screen. I felt a presence of someone being with me. All of those pictures were rolling very quickly and they showed my whole past life.

When the pictures were gone, I had the feeling that I had two personalities ... just like there were two of me. One was higher than the other. I know this sounds silly, but that is what I felt. I was dressed up ... how it happened I was dressed up so beautifully, I don't know. The clothing I had on was made of some very fine material ... it was generally white in colour with some silver and gold. I was able to travel forward in time and see all the situations of my life which I am now living in down here on Earth. I saw the whole of my future and travelled to different places to see different people. I was also observing my own person or my own human body going around and speaking to people. When my travelling as a soul was finished, I went back to my human body in bed and woke up. I can only say that Heaven is 'home'. There is someone waiting for me, but first I've got to finish my work down here.'

'This drawing will give you an idea of what my eyes have seen in the Universe'. Mrs Nyks

Operating room miracle

A car accident victim says her spirit hovered over her body during a desperate operation to save her life ... and guided the hand of the surgeon. Margarita Nomgard, 27, a nurse in Breda, Holland, says she died as doctors in Amsterdam frantically tried to stem bleeding from internal injuries resulting from the car crash. 'I suddenly realized that I was awake and looking down upon a team of surgeons and nurses. They seemed very upset and concerned about their patient. In a flash, I knew the patient was me, and that my soul had left my body. I remember feeling great love and pity for the poor people who were trying to save me. Then I knew that I was supposed to help them ... and I did', she says.

'I remember thinking that the surgeon was missing a deep cut that was bleeding badly in a ruptured kidney', said Margarita, who was interviewed by Beatrice Dexter in Amsterdam. 'I recall floating towards the operating table and coming closer towards him, placing my hand on top of his and guiding it towards the hidden cut. Suddenly he said, 'Oh, here it is ... here's the source of bleeding'. At that point my spirit re-entered my body and my next memory is waking up in the recovery room'.

Surgeon Dr DS Ashari said his patient was haemorrhaging badly until he repaired a deep laceration in her right kidney. 'There certainly was a very dangerous moment during the procedure, no doubt about it', Dr. Ashari said. 'At one point we lost her pulse, but once the hemorrhaging was stopped, she came right back'.

'I've been to the other side'

Kimberly Clark Sharp, 41, says a NDE 'changed my life like night into day'. Twenty years ago she collapsed while standing in a line. As an ambulance rushed her to a hospital, emergency workers accidentally hooked a ventilator to her backwards. Instead of pumping oxygen into her, it sucked all the air out of her lungs. 'My lungs collapsed and all attempts to revive me failed.'

She became engulfed by a blinding bright light. 'This light was God', she said. 'Any question I had, this light answered it completely. I was ecstatic. I wanted to stay there forever. But the white light told me: It's not your time. You have to go back and help others. I found myself back alongside my body in the hospital. I saw people thumping my chest. Suddenly I was back in my own body, and I was conscious'. After her recovery, Kimberly, who had just graduated from college with a teaching degree, decided to switch careers ... to become a social worker.

'I changed from being a shallow, materialistic, lazy 21-year-old girl to a social worker who has spent the last fifteen years at the bedsides of dying adults and children stricken with cancer. People say I'm good at it because I have absolutely no fear of death. Why? I've been to the other side and I know there is nothing to fear. My NDE was a miracle!'

Finally, there is a kind of physical courage that comes out in some of the accounts received. This is something that goes beyond mere risk-taking for one's own ambitions in life, but rather focuses on sacrifice for others.

One Indiana psychologist, who nearly died after a freak accident around her home, expressed this thought beautifully: 'You realize and appreciate how easy it is to be alive one moment and dead the next. I am really not afraid of death. I only don't want to die because I have too much to do on Earth and it would cause a lot of pain for family and friends. I would rather be one of the last to die so I don't cause too much pain for others'.

Accompanied by a glorious being

In his book, *Human Personality and Its Survival of Bodily Death*, FWH Myers relayed this remarkable experience of a railroad engineer in Jacksonville, Florida, who had an accident while unloading a railroad car:

'I saw a medium-sized person standing at my right hand clothed in white with a bright countenance, beaming with intelligence. I knew what he wanted in an instant, although he put his hand on my shoulder and said, 'Come with me'.

We moved upward, and a little to the southeast, with the speed of lightning, as it were. I could see the hills, buildings, trees, and roads as we went up side by side until they vanished out of our sight. As we passed on, this glorious being that was with me told me he was going to show me the bright heavenly world. We soon came to a world of light and beauty, many thousand times larger than this Earth, with at least four times as much light. The beauties of this place were beyond any human being to describe. I was seated by the tree of life on a square bunch of what appeared to be green velvet moss, about eighteen inches high. There I saw many thousands of spirits clothed in white and singing heavenly songs ... they were the sweetest sounds I have ever heard. I told my attendant that it was the first time I had ever been perfectly at rest in my life. They did not converse by sound, but each knew the other's thoughts at the instant, and conversation was carried on in that way, and also with me.

After viewing the wonderful beauties of the place for some time, and the thousands of spirits, robed in spotless white, passing through the air, for they did not confine themselves to the surface, but went every direction they pleased, I wanted to see my dear mother, two sisters, and a child of mine that had died sometime before this. The request was granted at once, but I was not allowed to converse with them. They were so youthful, standing in a row in front of me, and I looked at them and coolly estimated the distance we were apart at thirty feet. They seemed very much pleased to see me, and I shall never forget how they welcomed me when I first saw them, although no conversation passed.

About this time my attendant told me we must go back. I wished to stay, but he told me my time had not come yet, but would in due time, and I should wait with patience. At this we started back, and were soon out of sight of that heavenly land. Then we came in sight of this world. I saw everything as it looked from a great height ... till we came to the railroad car ... and I found myself there in the body, and he vanished out of my sight'.

'The day I was taken to my womb'

A young lady named Jennifer sent in this story from Perth, Western Australia after her experience in the late 1980s.

'One morning while in labour, I remember being taken out of my body and I could see myself lying there in my hospital bed with something across my stomach. God stood beside me and we went in (to my stomach) with the light from his face showing the way. I saw my baby in a bag of water, and as we came closer to her, I saw her moving around. She brought her hand forward and put it against the bag. I touched her little hand and could feel the little bumps. God then spoke to her and said, 'Put your head against the bag'. She did, and I kissed her cheek. Then she turned her head and looked at me. Everybody knows that baby's eyes are not open at that stage, but hers were. We then left my womb and moved up towards the ceiling. I then felt my spirit thump back into my body. I awoke and had a bad feeling that one of us was going to die. Forty-four hours after Sandy's (my baby's name) birth she died. I am glad that I was able to share such a beautiful experience a mother could ever have.

'Just two weeks after Sandy's death, I sat outside gazing into the night heavens wondering whether she is there yet ... and what happens when you die? Then I saw a bright light, it became clearer and an arched doorway appeared and slowly opened. In the background were many angels and one moved forward and spoke to me. He spoke to me but his mouth never moved. His voice went right into my heart and said, 'Jenny, I am coming for you'. He truly looked beautiful ... looking like a king, yet I could not see all of his face. Then he slowly disappeared. I couldn't make out what he meant.

'Towards the end of 1991 he appeared again in the arched doorway and again said that he was coming for me. One afternoon shortly after, I felt quite weak, and laid down on the bed, drifting into a twilight sleep. I felt my spirit leave my body and drift up to the ceiling. I looked down and I was still lying on the bed. My mouth was quite blue. I heard a voice say, 'Jenny, I have come for you as I promised'. I looked and there stood a glow of light and a figure slowly appeared. It was the angel, still looking like a beautiful king dressed in white flowing gown and a royal blue cloak. It too flowed, but I still couldn't quite see his face. I went closer to him and took his hand. He spoke to me and said, 'Jenny, look at you. You truly look like a princess'. I looked and I was also dressed in white and blue. I had long flowing hair and he was right ... I wore a crown upon my head. He touched my head and my crown glowed brighter. We went up to a dark tunnel and he said, 'Enter the tunnel of death, and be not afraid. Enter now and your guardian angel will meet you there, and take you through. I went on in ... it was dark, damp and cold with the running of water and a lot of mist. It was so long and it seemed to take a long time. Then I saw a light at the other end. An angel spoke and said, 'Come Jenny, I am your guardian angel'. We came closer to the light and came to the end of the tunnel. The angel then spoke and said, 'I am leaving you, now'. I looked at him and he just smiled at me. He touched my chin and said, 'Don't be afraid'. He looked beautiful. His face was so soft and his voice so gentle. His hair was long and flowing.

'A voice spoke from the light and said, 'Step into my light Jenny ... come and see how beautiful the valley of death is'. So I did and it truly was beautiful. The waterfall so tall and sparkling ... the hills in the valley were like a big blanket covering them with flowers. There was also a sweet fragrance in the air. An angel stood beside me with his right hand raised and said, 'Behold the valley of death in all its splendour'. Then we went on towards Heaven; a long stairway was there and we walked up it for a short time. Then the stairs disappeared and we stood at the Gates of Heaven. The gates opened and a big beautiful kingdom appeared. Then we walked through the gate. There were streets of gold for miles. Then we came to a door ... it too was made of gold. It opened slowly as we walked through and I saw God the Father. He wore a white gown also. But he wore a big crown and his hair was so soft and so white just like sheep's wool, but so white like snow. His eyes were like flames of fire and when he spoke my name, Jenny, thunder came out of his mouth and the heaven's shook and lightning bolts flashed from his mouth. But so much love came from his mouth and heart. He told me to come to him and I walked over. In Heaven you all move slowly. God reached out and said, 'Come, my child, come to your father in Heaven who truly loves you.

'He picked me up and sat me on his knee. His hand was so strong and yet so gentle. He pressed my head against his chest and told me to rest in his love. Then he put me down and raised both his arms and said, 'Let all of Heaven rejoice as one, for my daughter is home'. Then the angels appeared ... there were many of them. They sang so beautifully and the music was like you couldn't believe. Then the big golden doors opened again. Slowly in walked Sandy, Suzie and my mother in all their beauty and splendour. They walked towards me and God stood very close to me and said, 'Come and see Jenny'. Sandy saw me and touched my hand

and said, 'Hello mother'. Then my mother said, 'Jenny, I have always loved you', and she held me. Suzie came and gave me a big hug and said, 'Jenny, I love you and we all miss you'. Sandy took my hand again and God spoke with great love, 'You must go back now'. I said, 'But Father, I don't want to'. He just looked and said, 'Jenny you will be here with us very soon'. An angel hugged me and said, 'You must. Our Father wants you to share what you have seen.

'Then God spoke with great authority and the heavens shook and lightning came out of his mouth. 'My daughter Jenny will go back through the tunnel of death. The angel of death will leave his tunnel so she can return as I have instructed. Let no evil harm my child. Go my daughter and know I have ordered all evil to leave and to never harm you as Heaven goes with you'. I left through the big golden door. I turned and said, 'My Father in Heaven, I truly love you. I will never let you go out of my heart or love'. I waved to him and my mother and Suzie. Sandy was allowed to walk me to the gates of Heaven and then she stopped. I kissed her and held her tight. Sandy said, 'See you very soon, mother'. My guardian angel put his arms around my shoulder and said, 'It is time to go now'. We went back through the gate and down the stairs. Then to the tunnel of death and before we entered the angel spoke to the Angel of Death and said, 'You must not stand in our way. Be gone now'. With that there was a big black mist in the shape of an angel. He fled. My guardian angel came through with me ... we came to the end and I went back to my room. I was slightly fighting, saying I want to go back. 'No Jenny, not yet, but very soon. Tell the world what you've seen ... know Heaven is with you. With that my spirit was ordered back to my body. I felt a thump as my spirit went back. I woke up and felt cold and a little weak. I looked in the mirror and my lips and face were quite blue. But I soon warmed up and received my colour back'.

Mrs Stapleton's experience

Anita Stapleton had wondered many times whether there was life after death, then one night the ghost of a priest appeared before her and gave her the answer. The apparition provided Mrs Stapleton with details of his life on Earth more than a century earlier ... and she was able to prove that the priest had, in fact, lived. Here, in her own words, is her story:

'The day had been a normal one for me in my home in Labrador, Australia. I had gone about my daily chores, watched television in the evening, and finally went to bed while my husband was still watching the late movie on TV. The bedroom was not dark, because the bright light of a full moon fell through the window. I had just lain down, ready to go asleep, when I noticed that I was not alone. Right in front of the wardrobe, and looking straight at me, was a middle-aged man, dressed like a Catholic priest.

I rubbed my eyes and pinched my arms to make sure I was fully awake. The priest was still standing there looking at me. He was a frail man with hollow cheeks. His face showed traces of a hard life and illness. He looked so real, not like a ghost. I was not a bit scared, because he radiated vibrations of utter peace.

'Hello Father', I said. 'God bless you'.

'And God bless you, my child', he replied.

'He was well spoken, his voice soft. His English accent was not hard to distinguish. After stressing that there is survival after death, he told me he was Fredrick William Faber, and that he had lived in England from 1814 to 1863. When I remarked that at the time of his passing he was only 49 years old, he confirmed this and added that he had died of a kidney disease. After talking about religious matters for a few more minutes, he bade me farewell and disappeared.

'The incident troubled me for days ... how could I ever find out the truth? Then my husband reminded me of Somerset House in London where a record of every person born and deceased in Britain is kept. However, he did not know how far back these records went and Father Faber had been dead for over 100 years. Should I write to Somerset House? I hesitated. I did not want to make a fool of myself in case the whole thing was an hallucination.

'A few days later, however, I took the plunge and wrote requesting a search. Two weeks later an airmail letter arrived from Somerset House. Then I almost fainted. The letter contained a certified copy of a death certificate. It stated that Frederick William Faber's death had occurred on 26 September 1863, that he had been 49 at the time of his death and had been a doctor of divinity in Brompton, County of Middlesex. The cause of death was stated as kidney disease.

'The official document in my hands confirmed what the apparition had told me! Now I know for sure that there is life after death. To me it has been proved beyond the shadow of doubt'.

Coma boy visits Heaven

For three months Pietro Volpato lay in a coma in a hospital bed ... while his spirit was in heaven visiting with dead relatives. And when the 5-year-old boy awakened from his comatose state, he knew details about the lives of relatives who died before he was born, including a favourite song of his grandmother's that he had never heard before.

'I went through this big tunnel of light and went to a beautiful place, the Istrana, Italy', the child told his father, Luciano, when he came out of his coma. 'It was full of sunshine and music and I wanted to stay there. But they told me to go back to the other world because my mama and papa were waiting for me. I did what I was told to do'.

Psychologist Victor Milani is convinced that he did go to heaven. 'He never even met his grandparents but he correctly stated that his grandfather walked with a slight limp and had a habit of tugging at his ear when he talked. He also described an unusual birthmark that his grandmother had on her arm. I have spoken with the boy's father and I am convinced that he couldn't possibility have known these things unless he had, in fact, met his grandparents in heaven'.

Pietro was severely injured when he was stuck by a car while riding his bicycle. He was in a coma when he arrived at the hospital and doctors held out little hope for him. But day after day, week after week, the boy survived and his parents began to believe that he might make it. One morning while Luciano sat at his son's bedside, brown-haired Pietro regained consciousness.

'I have been in a strange place, Daddy', the boy said. 'It was Paradise and I met people who told me they have been dead for a long time. I was very happy there. It was always light there and I heard the sweetest music that followed me wherever I went'.

Pietro spoke over and over of his visit with his grandparents ... of the games they played with him and the songs they sang. He had learnt a favourite song of his grandmother's, a little lullaby in her native Neapolitan dialect which Pietro had never heard. 'I remember my mother singing the lullaby to me when I was a baby', said Luciano. 'I never sang it for Pietro yet he knew it word for word after he came back from his coma. Something happened in those three months he was unconscious ... something that proves to me that there is life after death'.

Predicting the future

Perhaps the most intriguing aspect of Margot Grey's book, *Return from Death*, (Routledge and Kegan Paul), has to do with planetary visions observed during clinical death ... ostensibly precognitive glimpses of coming world events.

Whatever one's interpretation of the evidence, there is a surprising consensus on what is to come: widespread earthquakes and volcanic activity, a pole shift, erratic weather patterns, drought and food shortages, economic collapse, social disintegration, diseases of unknown origin, and possibly nuclear or natural holocaust or catastrophe. Such calamities are seen as the inevitable result and reflection of a universally flagrant and ignorant violation of natural and spiritual laws, a necessary shake-up and purification which will bring a new sense of unity and co-operation. The severity of the disasters is said to depend on the extent to which human beings work to acquire the qualities that the NDE itself brings; unconditional love and spiritual values.

'A voice spoke to me'

The are large numbers of people who report that they have had special kinds of religious experiences, and these experiences are often characterized by mystical happenings similar to the near-death reports. For example, a middle-aged woman from Texas said that as she was driving down a mountain and rounded a curve in the road, 'I looked up to see a fast-travelling train coming out of the trees. Even though I wanted badly to slam on the brakes, I knew that there was no way to avoid being hit. So I screamed, 'What should I do?' A voice as clear as I have ever heard said, 'Put on the gas'.

'Going against my own will, I tried to beat the train ... and I was hit at the back door of the car but never got knocked off the highway and came to a stop on the shoulder of the road. As I opened my eyes, I believed surely that I was about to meet my Creator. But I felt surprise, then disappointment, then happiness to see that I was still alive and unhurt. Nearby workers said that if I had put on the brakes, the train would have hit me broadside and dragged the car down the tracks'.

In this case, the person was in great danger and came near death but was uninjured as a result of the incident. She felt that the near-death disaster brought her into touch with a life beyond this reality that in effect warned her and gave her specific directions that saved her life.

Deathbed scenes

There are certain happenings surrounding deathbed scenes that survivors have witnessed first hand, and these events add to our growing body of information about the other side of death.

A son reported that his mother, in the moments immediately before she died, looked upward and said, 'Oh, its so beautiful! There are steps leading to the golden Gates of Heaven'.

In another case a woman who was in the last seconds of her life looked up and in the presence of witnesses said, 'There's Bill, he is calling me in a clear loud voice', and then she passed away. As it happened, Bill was her brother and he had died just the week before ... but she had never been informed of his death.

CHAPTER 5

Life after near-death

Since the Near-Death Experience appears to be miraculous, it has acquired powerful religious overtones. Research now shows that there is a continuation of conscious experience in some 40 per cent of cases where a person's physical body is comatose after an accident, surgery or other life-threatening trauma. The subjective existence of the NDE is no longer in doubt nor are the sometimes dramatic after effects.

Perhaps the most pervasive after-effect of the NDE lies in the changed attitude to death and the possibility of an afterlife. Experiencers ... as distinct from people who have been close to death but have not experienced continuation of consciousness ... lose their fear of death and are convinced of the existence of an afterlife, whatever the researcher's conflicting interpretations.

They tend to find they have an enhanced appreciation of beauty, silence, the present and the small things in life. Their concern for others is greater; they have more tolerance and acceptance; they become more sympathetic listeners. They are less concerned with impressing others and have an increased sense of self-worth. Material values and status matter less so there is more emphasis on being rather than having. Some record the development of paranormal and healing abilities. There is a quest for meaning and intellectual or spiritual understanding. The change in religious or spiritual orientation can also be significant; typically, there is an emphasis on the spiritual life and unconditional love with less stress on formal aspects of religion.

People feel closer to God, especially if they have had a mystical encounter. There is an openness to Eastern religions and the idea of reincarnation, a belief in the essential unity of all faiths, and an intense desire for a universal religion which would dissolve the barriers that human beings have erected against each other. So the NDE is not a peripheral phenomenon of merely private interest. It points to a living universe and a spiritual view of humankind, towards personal survival of death and towards the breakdown and renewal of our civilization. The crisis is an opportunity.

The following two stories are typical of the changed attitude in people's lives after an NDE.

A gung-ho, combat-hardened marine became a mild-mannered lab technician after he was wounded in Vietnam, and almost died. This is just one of the people who have undergone transformations after having an NDE, according to a psychiatrist who has written forty articles on the subject. 'Studies show that eight million Americans have had an NDE and many of their experiences are similar', declared Dr Bruce Greyson, associate professor of psychiatry at the University of Connecticut Health Center. This is the account of Steve Price, 45, who is a member of a support group headed by Dr Greyson.

> I was flown to the Philippines to be operated on. While waiting to be wheeled into the operating room, suddenly I realized I was up near the ceiling, looking down at my body.

Then he passed through 'a brilliant white light' that seemed to embrace him and bathe him in the most peaceful, joyous feeling imaginable.

> I found myself in a place like the Garden of Eden. On the other side of a stream bubbling under a white bridge through the garden was my long-dead grandfather. I went to move towards him, but he waved me back. 'Steve, it's not your time yet', he said. And then I was back in a hospital room. My operation was over. The NDE had an incredible effect on my life. No matter how hard I tried, I couldn't fire my rifle. In 1972 I left the Marines and I now work as a lab technician. I'm now mild-mannered, thoughtful and a lot different from the hard-charging, macho marine I once was.

Joe Geraci, 47, also one of Dr Greyson's group, says: 'I was a no-nonsense hard-nosed cop for ten years. My NDE changed all that'. In 1977 he developed internal bleeding following an operation and his heart stopped beating as doctors worked to save his life.

> I felt the most total peace that I've ever felt', he said. 'I felt

a presence, a sensation of being with God. It was the most wonderful experience I've ever had.

Doctors got his heart beating again, but Geraci left the hospital a completely different man. 'After being a cop used to bloodshed, I found I couldn't watch TV because it was too violent!'

He quit the police force and now is a district co-ordinator for the public school system in New Britain, Connecticut.

CHAPTER 6

Children and death

Dying children can sometimes look through death's doorway and literally perceive the properties of the afterlife. Many children become extremely psychic when faced with death.

Dr Elisabeth Kubler-Ross is probably one of the world's best known and respected experts on the psychology of dying and death. The Swiss-born psychiatrist had previously been concerned primarily with people coming to the end of long and productive lives but in *Living with Death and Dying* she devoted a significant chapter to the care of dying children. Beginning in the late 1970s, she began refocusing her private practice, and became fascinated with the challenge of counselling these young patients. Her experience in specializing in their psychological care served as the topic for her best-selling book, *On Children and Death* which explores the psychological world of the dying child and its many facets. What is so surprising is that the book doesn't merely cover the psychological aspects of this inner world, but also deals in part with the dying child's psychic perceptions and experiences.

Parapsychologists have long known that some people become extremely psychic when faced with death. Children are no exception to this general rule. Please remember that death has been progressively robbed of its spiritual essence by the consistent mechanization of society, and today it is rare for a patient to return home to die.

People more commonly die in hospital rooms, often unconscious, and usually hooked up to several life support systems. Luckily, though, Dr Kubler-Ross refused to champion this impersonal approach and lack of regard for the dying person. She preferred to counsel the dying wherever they remain most comfortable, and she gradually rediscovered the psychic world of dying children through this practice. She reports openly about this inner world in *On Children and Death*. Children seem intuitively conscious of death and sense its presence whether it comes from disease or from sudden accident.

'One couple shared the story of their little eight-year-old girl who died from a freak accident during a trip overseas', reports Dr Kubler-Ross, 'and how they missed the clues that they might have been better off not going on the trip at all'.

The little girl was killed when she fell and struck her head. Her parents rushed her to a hospital, but the facility was several miles away and the child survived for only twenty minutes. Later the parents realized that their daughter had intuitively sensed her death. Even during the flight the child was seen writing a thank-you note to the family's (future) hosts. She had never written such a note before. She then gave the letter to her sister, asking the girl to deliver it in her stead. She seemed to realize that she wouldn't live to deliver the letter personally.

Remarkable, too, is a letter Dr Kubler-Ross received from a similarly distraught parent. Two days before her daughter was killed in a traffic mishap, the correspondent took the girl to dinner. During the meal they discussed their future and the girl's mother expressed some concern regarding her daughter's declining school grades. That's when the girl suddenly said that it didn't matter. 'My life is almost over', she explained to her startled mother. She expressed herself in a disarmingly matter-of-fact style.

What was even more bizarre was the way the girl obviously prepared for her coming death, since she left significant clues for her mother. 'She spent the last couple of days ironing everything', the mother wrote in her letter to Dr Kubler-Ross. 'I couldn't believe the order of her room; this is a fifteen year old child, you know. I was just amazed. And she didn't take any identification with her (the day of the accident), and so I see it as an act of love because she knew. She knew when she left to go in the car that she would not be coming home again; she didn't want me to be awakened at one in the morning to be told that my daughter had died, and I didn't find out until three o'clock the next day'.

These important comments become clearer when the entire letter is read. The child always took her ID with her when she left the house, so this singular oversight was significant in the mother's opinion. She left the ID by her bedside right next to her diary, and when her mother explored further she found an important passage inscribed in the book. The message was written for her benefit, and it exhorted her to self-heal the pain she felt. The girl obviously expected her mother to find the passage after her death.

Children's experiences with the afterlife

The fact that children are sensitive to the coming of death is not Dr Kubler-Ross's only discovery, for the psychic world of the dying child is more complex.

She cites additional cases where children suddenly began talking about death, reincarnation, and other spiritual issues just before life-threatening accidents. These cases do not always represent simple precognitions or intuitions of death though, for sometimes the children actually received some kind of spiritual revelation concerning their future state. The most sensational letter the psychiatrist ever received came from a parent on the East Coast and fits directly into this category. She explained to Dr Kubler-Ross that her daughter woke up early one morning in a state of extreme euphoria and excitement. She had slept in her mother's bed that night, and she woke her by spontaneously shaking and hugging the sleepy parent.

'Mom, Mom!' she kept saying, 'God told me I'm going to Heaven! I enjoy to go to Heaven, Mama, and its all beautiful and gold and silver and shiny, and God is there'. The girl was talking so quickly and excitedly that her mother could not remember the entire speech. 'I was affected mostly by her excitement', the correspondent wrote to Dr Kubler-Ross. 'My daughter was by nature a calm, almost contemplative child, extremely intelligent, but not a child much given to wildness, bounding-about-silliness that many four-year-olds get. She was verbally skilled and very precise with her speech. To find her so excited that she was stammering and tripping over her words was very unusual. In fact, I don't remember *ever* seeing her in such a state; not at Christmas, birthdays, or the circus'.

The mother tried to calm the child, but the little girl's enthusiasm couldn't be quashed. She kept talking of the angels, the jewels she saw in heaven, and the beings she would meet there. Finally, and almost in despair, the child's mother reasoned with her the best she could. 'If you went to Heaven, I'd miss you', she explained. 'And I'm glad you had such a happy dream, but let's slow down and relax a minute, OK?'

But the girl ignored her and kept talking about her experience. 'It was *not* a dream' she insisted, 'it was *real*'. She emphasized the claim in that dejected way that little children sometimes do. She said further that she would take care of her mother from heaven. This conversation continued for several minutes before the child finally relented, went out to play, and wasn't seen for the rest of the day. Sometime later in the afternoon the girl was found murdered. Her life came to its tragic end seven hours after she received the revelation.

The subject of dying children and their psychic world will probably depress many people. We usually feel bitterness when a child's life is so suddenly cut short ... either by accident or as a result of diseases such as leukemia, but I think there is a spiritually uplifting side to this dark picture. Dr Kubler-Ross's cases indicate that some power was preparing these children for their deaths, and the children seemed intent on sharing this information with their parents. In fact, this process of sharing seems to be a consistent feature of such cases ... i.e. death comes to those prepared for it. Though the murder was both tragic and senseless, the child openly welcomed her death and looked forward to her future life in the beyond. 'Shortly before children die there is often a very 'clear moment' as I call it', writes Dr Kubler-Ross in *On Children and Death*. 'Those who have remained in a coma since their accident or surgery open their eyes and seem very coherent. Those who have had great pain and discomfort are very quiet and at peace. It is in these moments that I asked them if they were willing to share with me what they were experiencing'.

A deathbed vision

The results of these inquiries eventually contributed to Dr Kubler-Ross's personal belief in spiritual immortality. The psychiatrist was summoned during one such crisis to the bedside of a traffic accident victim. The boy's mother was killed in the crash, but his brother Peter survived and was being treated in a different hospital where the facilities included a better burn centre. When Dr Kubler-Ross asked her charge whether he felt okay, the boy replied with a surprising comment. 'Yes, everything is all right now', he told Dr Kubler-Ross. 'Mommy and Peter are already waiting for me'. The little boy gave a contented smile and slipped back into a coma from which he failed to recover. 'I was quite aware that his mother had died at the scene of the accident, but Peter had not died', reports the psychiatrist. 'He had been brought to a special burn unit in another hospital, severely burnt, because the car caught fire before he was extricated from the wreck. Since I was only collecting data, I accepted the boy's information and determined to look in on Peter. It was not necessary, however, because as I passed the nursing station there was a call from the other hospital to inform that Peter had died a few minutes earlier'.

'In all the years,' the psychiatrist says in *On Children and Death*, 'that I quietly collected data from California to Sydney, Australia; from white and black children, Aboriginals, Eskimos, South Americans, and Libyan youngsters, every single child who mentioned that someone was waiting for them, mentioned a person who had actually preceded them in death, even if by only a few moments ... and yet none of these children had been informed of the recent death of the relatives by us at any time. Coincidence? By now there is no scientist or statistician who could convince me that this occurs, as some colleagues claim, as 'a result of oxygen deprivation' or for other 'rational and scientific' reasons'.

It is because these cases provide such impressive evidence that Dr Kubler-Ross believes in a life beyond death. She links the importance of deathbed vision cases to the many NDE reports she has collected from her patients ... i.e. people who journeyed into the next world during close brushes with death. This emphasis on the spiritual dimensions of the death experience is reflected in Dr Kubler-Ross's thinking in a third important way.

She does not hesitate to collect and publish purported cases of children who returned from death to comfort their grieving parents. She writes in her book, for instance, about a mother who returned home one day in total despair. Her little daughter had been sexually assaulted and killed shortly before, which struck fear in the small community where she lived. Her mother was lying down when a bright light suddenly came through her bedroom window. Within the light appeared her six-year-old child smiling radiantly. The figure disappeared within a few moments but the contact significantly comforted the mother. 'The sight filled her with such peace and love', says Dr Kubler-Ross, 'that she was in a much better mental condition after this incident than the rest of the still frightened community'.

Ultimate personal growth

Probably Dr Kubler-Ross's advice, which she repeats consistently in each of her books, is that society should learn to live with death. By accepting that death is more of a psychological potential than some sort of dark enemy, we can learn to let go of the dying and not encumber them with our own fears and denials. Perhaps we can learn to appreciate death as a final chance for our ultimate personal growth. The courage and spiritual fulfillment so many children find during the process of dying represents an important lesson for us. They don't seem to show fears so many of us display when facing the prospect of death. Dr Kubler-Ross has actually redirected us to a wise and ancient truth first pointed out in the Bible ... that when it comes to matters spiritual, children can sometimes be our best teachers.

Descriptions of Heaven ... from children who have been there

A little girl who lay clinically dead for three minutes awoke and gave doctors a vivid description of Heaven, saying that it was a fun and beautiful place where she sat on God's lap. She said that she had been led into Heaven by a golden-haired woman called

Elizabeth and taken to see God where she was asked, 'Do you want to go back and see your mother?' She was then revived and started to breath again. This 8-year-old drowning victim is one of countless children who've recounted similar tales of the hereafter ... and provided additional proof of life after death. 'These youngsters have all been clinically dead. They've all had a glimpse of Heaven and made a conscious decision to return to life', said Seattle pediatrician, Dr Melvin Morse, who has studied the life-after-death recollections of numerous children. Dr Morse said the accounts of young people who've 'died' and come back are especially important because kids are less likely to be influenced by notions of what Heaven should be like.

Other children in Dr Morse's study include:

• An 11-year-old boy whose heart stopped beating in the lobby of a Seattle children's hospital. 'He said he heard a whooshing sound and suddenly found himself floating to the ceiling, where he could see the doctors working over his body', Dr Morse said. 'He accurately described what went on in that room and identified who was in the room even though he was in cardiac arrest'. When a powerful electric shock restored his heartbeat, the boy recalled being 'suddenly sucked back into my body'.

• A 16-year-old boy whose heart suddenly stopped beating said he remembers travelling down a tunnel with bright lights all around him. 'I don't know where I was going, but I really wanted to get to the end of that tunnel', he said.

- A 6-year-old boy who suffered cardiac arrest on the operating table also found himself moving at high speed down a tunnel.

CHAPTER 7

Entrances to eternity

Although childbirth is generally regarded as a relatively safe procedure, there is still enough physical stress and danger associated with it to make it one of the most common entrances to eternity revealed in interviews. Here are some of the reports that were received:

* A middle-aged Oklahoma housewife who was in the process of giving birth to her third child, said, 'I was in hard labour from 2am until 2pm. I was yelling for a 'C section' just before Daniel was born, but my doctor said, 'Shut up'. 'I wanted to die of shame for yelling. I wanted to die more than anything! At that moment, I just popped out of my body and was about two or three feet above myself and everyone in the room. My doctor said, 'My God! My God!!'

'Someone moved to my side and pounded on my chest and I wondered why he was hitting my chest. Daniel was coming out and was handed to a nurse and wrapped in a blanket. I looked up and saw many beings waiting for me but not talking. We all knew each other's thoughts. This was very beautiful. I turned around and wondered about my husband and started to go out the door, but only floated through the door and down the hall to where he was standing in the passage with my eight-year-old daughter. They were fine and I went back to the birth room. The 'beings' were waiting on me to decide whether to stay with them or re-enter my body. It was *my* decision! I wanted to stay on the other side, but felt I should stay and raise my new baby until he was eleven years old'.

'Immediately, I popped back into my body. My boy is now thirteen years old, and I keep finding another project to start or finish before I leave again'.

Here are a few experiences reported during childbirth that purport to be glimpses of the eternal, supernatural dimension of reality.

• A 60-year-old Kentucky housewife said: 'When my daughter was born, I almost died. I saw a white cloud at the end of a tunnel and I just drifted away into it. It was so peaceful and I was really amazed when the doctor brought me back to life'.

• A 38-year-old Michigan mother said: 'After childbirth I went into shock because of the loss of blood, and I could see everything going on in the room, including my own body lying on the table. I could hear everything ... it was as though my spirit had left my body and was looking down on it'.

• A 32-year-old Oklahoma housewife suffered a miscarriage with serious results and extreme pain. She said, 'I saw God, and although I could not give life to my baby, I should rejoice in giving birth in spirit'.

• An elderly Philadelphia resident said: 'After the birth of my daughter, I was pronounced dead. It was as though I had died and went to heaven. I heard people talking and praying at the bed. When I got to Heaven it was like a cloud, and an angel told me to ask God if I could go back and take care of my baby. I walked down on steps of outstretched arms of angels and woke up. I was gone long enough for them to send a telegram and call the undertaker'.

CHAPTER 8

The tunnel of light

The much-publicized 'tunnel' experience ... an archetype of transition ... is a common feature of the withdrawal from earthbound existence. Time and time again Experiencers told of 'seeing' their bodies lying beneath them before being pulled rapidly through a high cylindrical passageway. Sometimes they describe the tunnel as being made of glass bricks of pastel colouring. They then discover they have left their physical bodies and cannot comfort and reassure relatives and friends who have been left behind. In most cases, however, the onset of strange and wonderful experiences soon dissipates all earthbound attachment.

The tunnel appears to serve as the channel of conveyance to the afterworld. Some people are met by 'guides' while still in transit and escorted deeper into the experience, but most people tell of travelling alone and merging with a variety of people at the end of the journey. Whoever receives the new arrival into the *bardo* ... a deceased relative or friend, a conductor, or a guide who has been watching over its 'charge' during the last life ... is often there to provide further guidance. Blinding light and overwhelming illumination, is the predominant feature of entry into the life between life. No earthly bliss can compare with the unalloyed ecstasy that engulfs all who cross the threshold. Love is everything. All-powerful rapture obliterates fear and negativity as the soul is reabsorbed into the undifferentiated oneness of existence.

Mrs Johnson, of Sydney, Australia, said:
'Its so bright, so beautiful, so serene. It's like going into the sun and being absorbed without any sensation of heat. You go back to the wholeness of everything. I didn't want to come back. Everything makes sense, everything is perfectly just. Its wonderful to know that love is really in control.'

The nature of this joyously profound revelation varies from person to person and appears to be modulated by personal experience, consciousness, and expectations. Many Experiencers find themselves enveloped in a brilliant vault of light which radiates sensations of blissfulness and peace. Others see shades and hues so glorious that the colours of the spectrum seem positively anaemic by comparison.

CHAPTER 9

Judgment day

'What have you done with your life?'

If there is a private hell in the NDE, it is the moment when the soul presents itself for review. This is when remorse, guilt and self-recrimination for failings in life are vented with a visceral intensity that produces anguish and tears on a scale than can be quite unsettling to witness.

The belief in judgment after death pervades every religious, philosophical, and mystical tradition ranging from the ancient Egyptian belief in the 'weighing of the soul' before a dead tribunal to Zoroastrian teaching that a bench of judicial spirits balances each man's fate in accordance with the quality of his life. Three relentless judges stalk Greek mythology and the idea of a divine trinity crops up in the philosophy of Lao-Tzu, is represented by the Trimurti of the Hindus, and was adopted in Christianity as the Father, Son and Holy Spirit.

While the symbols and nature of the Judgment drama differ from culture to culture, the purpose of the exercise is always the same: to assess the soul's performance and to chart its future course. The common state of human imperfection has always brought a sense of great foreboding to this intimate appraisal. The Bible refers to 'a certain fearful expectation of judgment' (Hebrews 10:27), while the *Song of Olaf Ostesen* from Scandinavian mythology warns, 'how great the sorrow of the soul ... where souls are subject to the cosmic judgment'.

The testimony of many Experiencers thoroughly endorses the existence of a board of judgment and enlarges on the rather sparse descriptions handed down from the old religions. Nearly all who have had an NDE have found themselves appearing before a group of wise, elderly beings ... usually three in number, sometimes four, and in rare instances as many as seven ... perceived in a variety of guises. Sometimes the life-review was said to have taken place in the presence of a 'Being of Light' or a 'Divine Presence' who asked them, in effect, 'What have you done with your life?' The judge or judges can be of indeterminate identity or they may take on the appearance of mythological gods or religious masters. Said one subject:

> My guide took me by the arm and led me to a room where the judges were sitting at a rectangular table. They were all dressed in loose white garments. I sensed their age and wisdom. In their company, I felt very boyish.

The members of this etheric tribunal are highly advanced spiritually and may have even completed their cycle of earthly incarnations. Knowing intuitively everything there is to be known about the person who stands before them, their role is to assist that individual in evaluating the life that has just passed and, eventually, to make recommendations concerning the next incarnation.

While incarnate, one's negative actions can be rationalized and repressed; there are always plenty of excuses available. In discussions on NDEs the emotions generated by these actions emerge raw and irreconcilable. Any emotional suffering that was inflicted on others is felt as keenly as if it were inflicted on oneself. In their emotional turmoil the Experiencers often perceive themselves as handicapped by their own wrongdoing. A man who had murdered his lover said he appeared before the judgment board with his own throat slashed. A mother who had inadvertently killed her own child saw herself in chains and a woman who could not forgive herself for an act of betrayal expressed her burden of guilt:

> My whole anima is convulsing with pain, remorse, sadness, guilt ... I cannot look up at the Three for sheer shame. Yet all around there is a glowing warmth of blue rays and peace, a peace I am unable to fathom ...

The 'peace' that this Experiencer felt in the presence of the judgment board is commonly experienced. The judges radiate a restorative, healing energy that abolishes any handicaps and assuages all guilt. The man with the injured throat was made whole again and the woman in chains was aware of the shackles falling from her wrists and ankles. Another Experiencer commented:

Just to be there in front of the judges made me fearful. But I soon realized there was no need to be afraid. They radiated a benevolent type of caring and my fear left me.

Rather than confirm the self-loathing and dissatisfaction of the contrite soul, the board of judgment expresses encouragement, pointing out where the life had been positive and progressive. It's as if they are saying, 'Come on now, your life wasn't *that* bad'. To justify this more balanced viewpoint, the judges preside over the life review.

For the purposes of self-assessment, the soul is confronted with an instantaneous panoramic flashback which contains every single detail of its life. The comments of the Experiencers is that the process is immediate and all-enveloping; an absolute reliving of the last life. Said one person:

> It's like climbing right inside a movie of your life. Every moment from every year of your life is played back in complete sensory detail. Total, total recall. And it all happens in an instant.

When happiness was thrown away

The review tells the soul more about the last life than the individual alone could ever hope to realize, even with full restoration of memory, and an entire world of which the individual was not aware is given expression. The larger picture is etched in vivid detail so that the soul realizes for the first time when happiness was thrown away or when thoughtlessness caused pain in another, or when some life threatening danger was just around the corner.

The soul absorbs every jot of meaning from this personalized videotape and this precipitates a rigorous exercise in self-analysis. This is the soul's moment of truth and, as it proceeds, the judges tend to remain in the background. They do not appear to act in the authoritarian manner suggested by cultural tradition. Rather, they behave more like loving teachers whose aim is to encourage their student to learn and benefit from past mistakes. The board of judgment frequently initiates discussion of critical episodes in the last life, offers retrospective counsel, and instills reassurance that each experience, no matter how unsavoury, promotes personal development.

The individual's hopes, friendships, ideals, aesthetic inclinations and mental processes all form part of the review. Emotionalism is kept to a minimum as the judges gently assist the soul in an objective understanding of its actions within the larger context of many lives. Only by observing karmic trends and patterns ... always difficult to discern within a single lifetime ... can the soul gain some measure of its progress on the long, long journey of spiritual evolution.

This picture-in-depth is recounted in a manner that suggests the information is being drawn from the videotape of total recall. Many people returning from a close encounter with death have described a panoramic, wrap-around, full-colour, three-dimensional vision of the events of their lives. Some go so far as to say that in the course of this panorama, every single day of their life was presented before them. This reported rapid panoramic review of one's life presented to the dying person graphically displays the good and bad things done in one's lifetime.

When people saw any selfish acts that they had committed, they felt extremely repentant ... and when gazing upon events in which they had shown love and kindness, they felt satisfaction. Dr Moody notes, 'that the result of the Judgment came not from the 'Being of Light' or the Judgment board who seemed to love and accept these people anyway, but rather from within the individual being judged'. One of Dr Moody's subjects reported in *Reflections on Life After Life:*

> I first was out of my body above the building and I could see my body lying there. Then I became aware of the Light ... just light ... being all around me. Then it seemed there was a display all around me and everything in my life just went by for review, you might say. I was really very, very ashamed of a lot of the things that I experienced because it seemed that I had a different knowledge, that the light was showing me what was wrong, what I did wrong. And it was very real.
>
> It seemed like this flashback, or memory, or whatever, was directed primarily at ascertaining the extent of my life. It was like there was a judgment being made and then, all of a sudden, the light became dimmer, and there was a conversation, not in words, but in thoughts. When I would see something, when I would experience a past event, it was like I was seeing it through eyes with omnipotent knowledge, guiding me, and helping me to see.
>
> That was the part that has stuck with me, because it showed me not only what I had done but *how what I had done had affected other people.* And it wasn't like I was looking

at a movie projector because I could *feel* these things; there was feeling, and particularly since I was with this knowledge ... I found out that not even your thoughts are lost ... every thought was there ... your thoughts are not lost ...

This situation can be regarded as being most unpleasant indeed, and it is no wonder that quite frequently people may come back from this, feeling that they need to make a change in their lives. Consider the following passages taken from interviews with three men:

1. I didn't tell anybody about my experience, but when I got back, I had this overwhelming, burning, consuming desire to do something for other people ... I was so ashamed of all the things that I had done, or hadn't done, in my life. I felt like I had to do it ... that it couldn't wait.

2. When I got back from this, I decided that I'd better change. I was very repentant. I hadn't been satisfied with the life I had led up to then, so I wanted to start doing better.

3. A self-employed Californian man reported: While under water in a bay off the Philippines, having surfaced three or four times calling for help, I went through a desperate struggle to resurface. This was followed by a sequence of events relating to my life in high quality pictures, like a fast movie flashing in my eyes. It was all revealing and I felt terrible about some of things I had said to people. Then I must have collapsed. The next thing I knew I was lying on

the dock with several people around me, and one person attempting to revive me through artificial respiration. I became ill, but within an hour or so, I was fully recovered.

In the state that they were in, they seemed to have been shown for themselves what they should and shouldn't have done in their lives and then judged themselves accordingly.

You be the Judge

Many people stated that even for a period of time following their experience of the life-review, they could recall the events of their lives with incredible detail. Following is a representative account of what some correspondents reported seeing while they were clinically dead:

> • My every thought and deed of my lifetime was portrayed in a rapid three-dimensional panorama. I felt as if everybody around me knew my every thought.

> • I now realize that the beauty of the physical body or the colour of the skin can no longer be a source of pride. The beauty is within the soul.

> • All of my faults were revealed so very graphically in front of me. Now that I have been given the chance to live again, I am urgently trying to correct past mistakes.

> • I could see all the mean things I did as a child. I was a real mean little kid! I wished that I hadn't done those things

and wished I could go back and undo them. I sincerely apologized to my mother and father when I was revived.

• The best thing I can compare it to (the life-review/ judgment) is a series of pictures, like very high quality colour slides. It was just like someone was clicking the slides on and off in front of me, very quickly. It was all so fast.

• My whole life just flashed across my mind ... it was very quick. I saw myself crying as I went to school in the first grade. I was wearing a horrible pair of long shorts that were far to big for me ... it was very, very real and I was there!

• Certain events in my life were put in front of me so that I would have to recall them. I was actually walking through them ... everything was so fast, yet it was slow enough that I could take it all in. It was an overwhelming experience.

• Then the Judgment was put on and I was the Judge. This is a very crucial way of judging people because the harshest judge you can have of everything you do, is yourself. You are harsher on yourself than you are on anyone else.

• I was watching my whole life being replayed just like on a colour TV set. I felt great remorse for some of the bad things I had done in my life. This was my Judgment Day, I thought, and was I suffering; boy oh boy, was I suffering.

The data presented in this section indicates that the life review/judgment is a common experience encountered at the point of near-death. In each of these cases, the life review was an early event in the NDE and was perceived as having taken place outside the physical body, and ended with a feeling of having returned to the body.

CHAPTER 10

Planning the next life

The most significant finding of Dr Whitton's research is the discovery that many people sense that they need to eventually plan their forthcoming lives while discarnate. The knowledge of self, gleaned from the review process, equips the soul to make the vital decisions that will determine the form of the next incarnation. But the soul does not act alone. The decision-making is heavily influenced by the members of the Judgment board who, mindful of the soul's karmic debts and its needs for specific lessons, give wide-ranging counsel. Some Experiencers became aware that they were to write a karmic script for the next incarnation on Earth, complete to choosing their own mothers and fathers. In the Christian tradition, Jesus Christ is seen as the only incarnate being granted the privilege of choosing his parents. The NDE, however, shows that option is open to all and that the choice of one's parents, in establishing the setting and direction of the lifetime to come, is immensely important. The ancient Tibetans were well aware of this selection process, the *Bardo Thödol* advising the discarnate soul: 'Examine where you are going to be born and choose the continent'.

The judges' recommendations are made according to what the soul needs, not want it wants, so they tend to be received with mixed feelings unless the soul happens to be fanatical about pursuing its development at any cost. Said one woman:

> I am being helped to work out the next life so that I can face whatever difficulties that come my way. I don't want to take the responsibility because I feel that I don't have the strength. But I know we have to be given obstacles in order to over come those obstacles ... to be become stronger, more aware, more evolved, more responsible.

The price of advancement is always challenge and difficulty ... the very reason why incarnations become progressively more arduous as the soul evolves. Planning for the next life is frequently undertaken in consultation with other souls with whom bonds have been established over many lifetimes, which is to say the choice of the time and place of birth is of paramount importance; to choose wrongly is to miss the opportunity for a productive reunion.

The karmic script

The 'karmic script' often calls for renewed involvement with people who have figured, pleasantly or unpleasantly, in previous incarnations. In the words of one who felt compelled to make compensation to others:

> There are people I didn't treat too well in my last life, and I have to go back to the Earth plane again and work off

that debt. This time, if they hurt me in return, I'm going to forgive them because all I really want to do is go back home. This is home.

It would seem that the term 'soul-mate' relates to an entity with which one has purposefully reincarnated many times in the cause of mutual growth. But growth is just as often independent upon reunification with those whose company is not so exhilarating. 'Oh no, not her again!' groaned one subject, a high school teacher, on being told his personal evolution would be best served by being reborn to a woman he had murdered in a previous life.

CHAPTER 11

Celestial music

Exquisite, divine music coming from 'no-where' and appearing to be sung by vast choirs of singers in huge stadiums is often reported by people after revival from a close brush with death. This beautiful music has been described by some as a 'celestial symphony' produced by the spinning of the planets and other heavenly bodies. The percipients usually claimed that the sounds surpassed even the music of the great Romantic masters, and that it invariably faded into the distance as if the celestial musicians were floating higher into the heavenly realms. Some incidents have been reported in which several people heard the music in a dying person's room.

Dr Scott Rogo, in his publication *Beyond Reality,* notes that 'the belief that our purely terrestrial music is based on some sort of 'cosmic' harmony generated by the Universe or sent to us by God is of long standing, and similar doctrines emerged from several early cultures'. The belief that the heavens produce their own personal music is not merely a Western philosophical tenet, for the same concept crops up in Eastern philosophy as well.

According to some schools of yoga, there exists a stream in the Universe that expresses itself through cosmic sounds called *Nad* or *Nada*, into which a person can enter during meditation. Mr Raymond Bayless, a colleague of Dr Rogo, prepared this report of a description of an incident in which he personally experienced the phenomenon of 'the music of the spheres':

> One evening I had gone to bed and was still awake and fully conscious (I was about thirteen years of age), I heard in the distance the sound of what I believed to be a radio playing. At first the music ... at the beginning I realized that it was music I was hearing ... was barely heard, but it steadily gained in volume until it was clearly and distinctly heard, and then it diminished until it faded out completely. It was impossible to estimate the duration of the incident but I would guess that no more than a few minutes actually passed. It was also impossible to locate the music in space.
>
> I was interested in music greatly, but at the time possessed no 'formal' knowledge of type or origin. Despite this lack, I became completely aware that the music was totally unearthly and inconceivably beautiful and majestic. The greatest music on Earth, be it Brahms or Bach, is nothing but an inharmonious jangle of crude sounds by comparison. It was literally celestial and at the time I believed it to be associated with religious matters, and I still believe this to be so. It seemed to be produced by a vast number of players, singers; I do not know, but it was instrumental; it was on an inconceivably higher level than such distinction, and all that can be said is that it was

incredibly beautiful, clearly superhuman, and could not possibly originate from earthly instruments and voices. In spite of the time that has passed ... I am almost forty-nine ... the memory of the experience is powerful and unforgettable.

Some additional experiences are extracted from Dr Rogo's files and include this account from Mr Von Sealay who said:

It was approximately during the mid-1930s as near as I can remember. I was very much the materialist at the time ... a complete disbeliever in anything psychic, spiritual, or religious. I was walking down a hill smoking a cigar when suddenly I began to hear faint music in the distance. However, instead of actually being in the distance it was in my ears, in both ears, sounding as a stereo does today ... it seemed to be in my head. I just stood still and the music welled up into my consciousness; this is the only way I could describe it. I became overwhelmed by it. I could not distinguish any particular musical instruments or any particular melody and I could not identify any human voices. I just stood there and the tears came into my eyes and I think that I became entranced, for at least ten minutes. I was oblivious to a crowd of people around me but I only became aware of them when I recovered from this state. There is no way of describing the music except to say that I was overwhelmed by something so majestic that any music heard here on Earth is nothing, absolutely nothing in comparison to it.'

In another case:

> It was very early one summer's morning that I heard the
> music. I had, if memory serves me, slept very soundly, as
> was usual with me. But suddenly I was awake and there
> was music, wonderful music, coming in through the open
> window in the room. The room was on the first floor of a
> small house. Others in the house were asleep. All was quiet
> within. I got up, went to the window, and knelt before it
> looking into the morning light. I saw the large house across
> the way, perhaps fifty feet. A widow and her daughter lived
> in this house. Neither cared for music. The music could
> not have come from there. It came from the air outside
> the window. It poured in, seemingly against my face as
> though some of the musicians were as close as ten feet
> from me ... or so it seemed at the time and so it seems in
> the memory.
>
> I felt spellbound ... I did not try to move. But I listened,
> and this is what I heard: *A very large group of
> instruments being played in a way I had never heard
> music played before.* It was as though the instruments
> were not far apart, but close together, at least that is the
> impression I got.

Speaking retrospectively, Mrs Grace Russell of Edmonds,
Washington State, tried to describe the mysterious essence of
the music that she heard:

> I have thought about this music with sincere effort, trying
> to decide what instruments must have played it, but I never

came to a conclusion other than I did not know then and do not now. No one instrument played solo at any time. All played in unison. All played as one. But I felt there were many because of the variety of the tones. There were no wild clashes of sound, no beating of drums, no shrill high tones. There was a definite melody, wonderful harmony. Back of the melody, which seemed an endless song without words, I heard a deep roaring sound something like the ocean's roar. This was not louder than the rest, but it was there. The melody seemed to be carried by a great many instruments of high pitch expertly played. This music was of an intensity most unusual. It had meaning and great beauty. Not charm as some music, but a beauty that enthralled me.

Beautiful singing

One of Dr Rogo's favourite published reports concerned the clinical death experience of a British gentleman named John Britton, an intelligent, but deaf mute witnessed dying in his family home from rheumatic fever.

Because his hands were extremely swollen, he could no longer signal to his relatives, and every one expected him to die. The patient's brother-in-law, Mr S Allen, joined the household vigil when the family doctor summoned him. He was the first person in the household to hear the music, when he and his wife heard beautiful singing while staying in the room directly below Britton's chamber. They determined that it came from upstairs but could find no normal source for it.

Mr Allen later stated in writing:

> We found Jack lying on his back with his eyes fixed on the ceiling, and his face lighted up with the brightest of smiles. After a little while Jack awoke and used the words 'Heaven' and 'beautiful' as well as he could by means of his lips and facial expression. As he became more conscious he also told us in the same manner that his brother Tom and his sister Harriet were coming to see him. This we considered very unlikely as they lived some distance off, but shortly afterwards a cab drove up from which they alighted. They had sent no intimation of their coming, nor had anyone else. After Jack's partial recovery, when he was able to converse upon his fingers, he told us that he had been allowed to see into Heaven and to hear the most beautiful music.

The fact that the witnesses 'saw' his relatives coming implies that he experienced some sort of out-of-body experience, which he obviously survived.

The original records of this case were collected by Rev. LA Milford, the master of Haileybury College, who turned them over to the Society for Psychic Research. Since both the primary witness and his wife heard the music, it is difficult to maintain that Mr Allen's perceptions were simply hallucinations.

Some of the cases Sir William Barret included in his *Death-bed Visions* read even more impressively, since occasionally several people have reported similar music from such deathbed scenes! The physicist even published the statement of a physician who heard the music while waiting for an elderly patient to expire.

Dr Robert Crookall sent a further remarkable report to Dr Rogo from Great Britain. This report had been previously sent to him by Mrs Kathleen Snowden, who's musical out-of-body experience took place when she was a teenager:

> I was only sixteen years old, ill in bed. I told my mother that I thought I was going to faint ... I felt myself drifting away from her. Suddenly I realized a feeling of great excitement, wonder and delight surpassing anything I had ever experienced as I felt my body weightless and floating upwards in a golden glow towards a wonderful light around hazy welcoming figures and the whole air was filled with beautiful singing.

> I floated joyously towards the voice and the light and then I heard my mother's voice calling me ... my whole being revolted against going back. Her voice grew nearer and to my great distress, I felt myself slipping away from the wonderful light and merging into a dull black cloud where my heaviness of body returned ... my mother thought that I had died; I seemed to stop breathing ... I am now forty-two and the wonder of it still remains.

In my own research many people personally described similar incidents from their own lives. A woman who taught music experienced sound of staggering virtuosity. 'The compositions were incredible', she said. 'This was music that the world's greatest composers could only hope to emulate'. Some of their experiences were simple, straightforward events where 'logical' explanations just don't seem to fit. The following accounts are a summary from people who have undergone the experience of hearing divine music.

• As soon as the music began I could hear a remarkable difference from what I had been accustomed to here on Earth. The actual sound made by the various instruments was easily recognizable as of old, but the quality of tone was immeasurably purer and the balance and the blend were perfect.

Mrs LB, retired school teacher, Casino, NSW, while critically ill in hospital

• Unlike our music which can only be heard, there I had both *heard* and *seen* it. Not only was I inspired by the sounds of the orchestral playing, but the beauty of the immense form it created had a spiritual influence on me as I came into its sphere.

Mrs HJJ, accountant, Hallam, Victoria, after revival from a heart attack

• There was pandemonium of silver-toned music going on unremittingly. The sounds appeared to be in perfect accord with the colours. Where I went to, all music is colour and all colour is music. It was a place of beautiful light that pulsated with exquisite music. The world split ... everything was silver ... like diamonds and stars. The music reached a climax and then slowly softened. Suddenly, I

was back in my body and was very sorry for it.
Mrs C S, secretary, Toowoomba, Qld, after waking from a coma due to a horse-riding accident.

• I have heard transcendent music numerous times. One of the richest was an enormous choir of soldiers. You hear and feel the music ... it is a very living experience. Twice I heard a fantastic calliope.
Mr ALB, retired. After revival from a heart attack in an ambulance.

Whatever its nature, the 'music of the spheres' makes a considerable impression on the people who hear it. Their reports represent but a dim shadow of what the music must really sound like. One of Dr Rogo's subjects probably summed up her reaction to the music the best, for she explained that she would gladly die just to hear those harmonies of heaven for the second time. Perhaps each of us will personally hear these rapturous sounds when we make the great spiritual transition.

CHAPTER 12

Pets and the afterlife

In a world of animal lovers, the death of a dog, cat or pony can cause as much distress as the loss of a human relation. However, it seems that the spirits of pets survive after death ... and we are reunited with our favourite pets when we die, researchers claim. 'There is a good deal of exciting evidence to show that life after death exists for animals as well as humans ... and that we are reunited with our pets', declared Ian Currie, author of the book, *You Cannot Die.*

Brad Steiger, a leading reincarnation researcher and author of many books on psychic phenomena, said, 'The evidence is indisputable: Just as there is life after death for humans, so animals live on, too. They become our constant, loving companions beyond the grave'.

The two experts described séances at which the spirits of dead people revealed the joy they felt after they had been reunited with their pets. 'In one séance, a medium was in contact with a Frenchman who died some years earlier', recalled Currie. 'The man said that as soon as he died he felt the body of an animal nestling against him. When he opened his eyes, there was his pet horse, which had died before him'. On another occasion, a clairvoyant was in contact with a woman who had died. The woman said that within minutes of her death she was happily romping with her dog which had been killed by a car several years earlier. She said that the dog was in perfect shape. Steiger recalled a séance at which a dead woman described her reunion with a pet after she died; 'Suddenly when I opened my eyes, there on my lap, gently purring, was my pet cat, which had died some years earlier. I hugged and squeezed him and he nestled his head against my face. It was so comforting to have him there'.

Reunited with a horse

People returning from a close encounter with death have also reported seeing their deceased pets alive and well on the 'other side'. Nothing surprised or delighted them more than being greeted in the next world by their domestic animals or pets. Spouses and parents were sometimes expected, but Rover racing around in circles was a bonus.

George Wilmot, a rag and bone merchant and a drop-out from marriage being parted from two wives, recalled his astonishment at being greeted by his old horse during his NDE. 'The first thing I remember when I woke up over there was sitting in a lush field under a tree. I looked up and saw a horse coming towards me, and it was old Jenny! She used to pull my cart in earlier years, in my thirties. I was real upset when poor old Jenny collapsed and died. She was as near to me as any woman could be, in fact more so. I had great affection for her ... she knew everything that I ever said to her ... I'm sure she did. She was as cute as they come. She wasn't much to look at, I suppose, as horses go, of course, but she was a real nice old nag.

She looked younger of course, and she was so thrilled and so happy, you could sense and feel it ... I can't say how. But it was almost as if she was talking to me ... it was extraordinary. I couldn't hear any voice and you don't expect to hear a horse speak, but she was somehow mentally talking to me, I suppose. She was welcoming me and came beside me and was licking my face. Goodness me, I'll never forget this as long as I live. I was so thrilled and excited, and patting and fussing her'.

My deceased Dalmatian is alive and well

'It was a simple enough occurrence', wrote Jenny Jones. 'I'd finally gone to bed, curled on to my side with no hope of sleep, when a familiar bulk settled into the small of my back. I put a hand down to touch, but nothing. No furry coat, no cold nose, no velvet ear, no Lola. Yet the pressure was there, real enough, and stayed half the night. Only subsequent events convinced me that she was actually there.

Her death had seemed so unkind. She was barely nine years old. My first dog, the realization of childhood dreams and, in reality, a much adored companion, loved by all, who graced my life with a presence and beauty which, even now, I miss in the most extraordinary fashion.

Her death sentence had contained two chilling phrases. 'A rapidly failing heart', and 'inoperable lung cancer'. She was given a couple of weeks to live. With devotion, will power and a great deal of money I attempted to stretch those weeks. But I believe that it was mostly Lola's own determination not to leave those she loved best, which kept her going for almost a year.

The end was stunning. It was Mother's Day, which seemed sadly ironic as I always referred to myself as her Mum. She and I sat listening to music that evening, her wasted but still proud and beautiful body draped across my knees.

It was quick. It was clean. It was heartbreaking. Lola was suddenly dead in my arms. My Lola, gone. My Dalmatian. The light of my life. And if that sounds clichéd I can only apologise for stating an elemental truth.

The following morning saw Lola's burial and that bore an extra sadness because I was in the process of moving house and knew that within mere weeks I would have to leave her body behind. Hearts can't really break ... can they? I thought mine had.

The second time she visited I was more receptive, less disbelieving. I'd gone to bed early. Lola's daughter, Tully, was keeping me company and when she made a show of staring towards the door, she was obviously anticipating somebody's arrival. I naturally assumed that either my husband or daughter approached. But neither appeared. Tully, meanwhile, was wagging her whole body with delight and, watching her eyes, I too was able to follow a path around the foot and coming to rest by my husband's pillow.

Tully was on the bed and leaned forward and down, sniffing with apparent glee, her tail whipping the air frantically as she emitted small cries of pleasure. I could only assume that she saw what I did not. It seemed perfectly natural that it would be Lola, her mother.

A few days later sunshine invited me out of the house and I sat on a bench overlooking the front garden. I was deeply unhappy, still missing and mourning my very dear friend, and when something blurred appeared before me I assumed I'd got dust in my eyes. I blinked rapidly and when I refocused, there, on the path before me, was a startling sight. It was a group of dogs. Strangely I felt no real surprise, it seemed logical that they too should enjoy the sunshine. Anna was clearly visible. An old, blind, black Labrador who I'd rescued and whose death had occurred two years before. She sat on the path looking placid and overfed, exactly as she did in life.

Alongside reclined Lola. Not some misty see-through apparition but a clear vision, well-defined, substantial, her black spots glinting dully in the sunshine. Tears found me then.

Behind Lola stood Rowdy, another Dalmatian no longer with me. A tragic loss at less than one year of age, still missed, still fondly remembered. Also there, gambolling around the still adults, some small Dalmatian puppies. As a breeder I inevitably lost the odd pup and I believe it was they I saw.

There was another dog, less detailed as I observed her through a cloud. It was little Sue, a small brown mongrel, another of my rescues, dead for almost six years. The image stayed complete for perhaps three minutes before it wavered, blurred again, almost as if in a heat haze, then it simply disappeared.

I could have imagined the whole thing. Lola and Anna both loved that particular spot for sunbathing and the recent death had brought to my mind other similarly sad memories. But within the fleeting picture was a proof that I craved, enough to convince me. For another dog had appeared, I saw him well. Another Dalmatian and one I didn't recognize, certainly not one of mine but there nonetheless. It was then that I knew, with no lingering doubts, this was no fantasy. Dogs DO have ghosts! After that I expected to see Lola everywhere. Perhaps I wanted it too much, looked too hard, for nothing happened.

Time moved on and it was suddenly the night before the house move. Accompanied by my husband I went to Lola's grave to say a last goodbye. We talked to her, as we had in life, and as odd as it might sound I told her where we moving to, passing on the new address, adding: 'If you can't make it alone, come with me in the car'. I always intended to say a last goodbye on my own but my buyers and their removal men arrived ahead of time and I beat a hasty retreat, too embarrassed to have my last few minutes of memories observed by strangers.

I drove away from Lola and my old home with tears coursing down my face, consumed with guilt at leaving her body behind, feeling as if I abandoned her. I wondered if her spirit, or whatever still lived of her, would remain with her body.

The following days were emotional. I loved my new home and the other dogs were delighted with the extra space and land. But each time I watched them careering across the fields I was reminded of Lola who I so wanted to make the move with me. So many times before her death I'd imagined her bouncing across these new fields, whole and well. It was hard to accept she never would now.

Two months passed before I saw Lola again. I'd already given up hope, supposing that strong images did indeed stay at the burial site. But one evening as I watched television, I looked across at my husband who sat on the settee reading. She was so clear and alive that at first I couldn't comprehend that the dog lounging beside him, leaning on his arm, was Lola. I wrongly assumed it was one of the others but my eyes seemed drawn back and it was she.

I don't know how long I watched. She looked so happy and well but somehow I sensed that if I spoke or moved she would disappear. So the first hint of anything untoward to my husband was when he glanced up and saw not Lola but the tears on my face. As I tried to explain the image faded but I was ecstatic. All my guilt for leaving her body evaporated, to be replaced by a certainty that as long as she was talked about, loved and remembered, she would remain with us.

I've only seen her once since then. Perhaps I don't need to any more, though I miss her dreadfully, every day, every night. But the last time was a little strange, more in keeping perhaps with the stereotyped image we have of ghosts.

I awoke in the middle of the night as my husband was en route to the bathroom. He put no lights on and when I heard the loo flush, I too got up. We passed in the bedroom doorway and as he walked through he was preceded by a bouncing Dalmatian. I couldn't see her clearly, just a shining whiteness dancing past which looked ethereal and misty. But it was Lola. I'd have recognized that bounce anywhere. She was still with us!

In my first draft of this article the story ended there but a recent conversation with a friend prompts me to add just a little more.

She was talking of the time, some months before, when she had visited my husband in hospital. He was there for a lung operation and it was a time when he felt both vulnerable and, as we all do in such places, very much alone. My friend told me how astonished she'd been to see that the ward had a resident dog. Puzzled, I asked her to elaborate and she told me upon entering the ward she'd seen a dog lying on my husband's bed with its head on his chest. As she approached the dog jumped off and walked away without looking back.

I assured her that dogs were certainly not allowed in a cardiothoracic unit where the fight against infection is so crucial. Knowing the answer before I posed the question, I asked anyway, 'What sort of dog was it?' 'Oh', she replied, 'it was a lovely spotty dog like those of yours. A Dalmatian'.

CHAPTER 13

The negative Near-Death Experience

Some investigators of the NDE say that not all experiences are positive ones, and if there is a Paradise as is so often described, it would seem that a Hell would exist of necessity. It goes without saying that for a paradise to *be* a paradise, those who would make it less than heavenly would have to be excluded from it. It is hard to imagine a Heaven with Roman centurions, medieval Inquisitors, Argentine jailers, German Nazis, African dictators, or Arab terrorists etc. Any society which has an identity *as a society* must exclude those who do not harmonize with its purpose and who would corrupt or defeat it if they had a chance. It is difficult to imagine the Catholic church admitting anti-Catholics or the Masonic Lodge admitting anti-Masons and it is impossible to imagine Heaven admitting anti-socials. If such persons have a share in life after death, there must be a separate place for them and that is exactly what some Experiencers have described.

In a book called *Beyond Death's Door,* Dr Maurice Rawlings revealed that many of the stories relayed to him were most unpleasant indeed. One of them involved a middle-aged patient of his, a heart attack victim who 'died' several times in rapid succession in Dr Rawlings' presence, and claimed that he had been to Hell. Dr Rawlings then began to interview other resuscitated patients and he says that they reported two kinds of Near-Death Experience, not just one. There are the usual visions of beautiful landscapes and cities of light, but there are others as well, 'inexpressibly horrible, frequently a dungeon or huge cave'. 'These patients', he said, 'entered a dark passage just like the luckier ones, but instead of emerging into bright surroundings they enter a dark, dim environment where they encounter grotesque people lurking in the shadows ... the horrors defy description and are difficult for them to recall'. He likens Hell, as described by his patients, to 'a carnival's spook house' and believes that these experiences are just as common as the good ones. They often go unreported, perhaps because a trip to Hell is not something one freely talks about. It is possible, Dr Rawlings points out, that the experiences are so terrifying that the mind is unable to deal with them, and therefore represses and forgets them shortly after they are over.

In *Return from Death*, Margot Grey found it possible to discern five NDE stages which don't correspond to the positive ones: fear and a feeling of panic; out-of-body experience with an urge to return to the physical body; entering a black void; sensing an evil force which tries to drag you down; and entering a hell-like environment. Loneliness and desolation are the typical sensations; there is a sinking rather than a rising feeling, and unpleasant smells rather than sweet fragrances.

One Australian man I spoke to says he was 'pulled down by the ankle to an awful place' and that he expected to be 'in the deep' for some time, 'a penalty for breaking the rules'. He reported gruesome beings trying to grasp his torso and pull him deeper in the experience.

Dr Raymond Moody found these experiences existed mainly with people who had attempted to commit suicide but were revived. People commit suicide to escape earthly problems, but instead of oblivion they report finding themselves completely conscious and in a more dreadful place than the one they left. Moody says that 'in their disembodied state' the suicides he interviewed 'were unable to do anything about their problems, and yet they had to view the unfortunate consequence which had resulted from their acts'. 'The thing was', said one suicide victim, 'the problem was still around, even when I was 'dead'. And it was like it was repeating itself, a rerun. I would go through it once and at the end I would think 'Oh, I'm glad that's over'... and then it would start all over again'. In other cases, the obsession involves the act of suicide itself. In his visions, the suicide 'dies' as the Wandering Jew wanders ... endlessly.

British author Charles Williams describes these experiences in some detail in *Descent into Hell*, and since he was a member of the Hermetic Order of the Golden Dawn, and an experimenter in things psychic, it was believed that his descriptions were based on an actual experience that he called 'the purgatory of suicide'.

Descriptions of Hell

Emmanuel Swedenborg, in his book, *Heaven And Its Wonders, and Hell*, provided an extensive description of what the Theosophists call *Kama Loca*, or the 'lower astral plane'. Some Hells present an appearance like the ruins of houses and cities after conflagrations, in which infernal spirits dwell and hide themselves. In the milder Hells there is an appearance of rude huts, in some cases alongside the form of a city with lanes and streets, and within the houses are spirits engaged in unceasing quarrels, enmities, fights and brutalities; while in the streets and lanes robberies and depredations are committed. In some of the Hells there are nothing but brothels, disgusting to the sight and filled with every kind of filth and excrement. Again, there are dark forests, in which infernal spirits roam like wild beasts and where, too, there are underground dens into which those flee who are pursued by others. There are also deserts, where all is barren and sandy, and where in some places there are ragged rocks in which there are caverns, and in some places, huts. In these desert places are those who are cast out from the hells who have suffered every extremity of punishment, especially those who in the world have been more cunning than others in undertaking and contriving intrigues and deceits. Such a life is their final lot.

Emmanuel Swedenborg described the dwellers in Hell as 'all spirits, when seen in any light of Heaven, appear in the form of their evil ... It is impossible to describe how all these forms appear, for no one is like another, although there is a general likeness among those who are in the same evil ... In general, their faces are hideous, and void of life, like those of corpses. The faces of some are black; others fiery, like torches. Still others are disfigured with pimples, warts and ulcers. Some seem to have no face, instead something hairy or bony, and with some only the teeth are seen. Their bodies are monstrous, and their speech is like the speech of anger or of hatred, or of revenge ... But it must be understood that this is the way infernal spirits appear in the light of Heaven, while among themselves they appear as men. As soon as any ray of light is let in, their human forms appear changed into monstrous forms ... for in the light of Heaven everything appears as it is. For this reason they shun the light of Heaven and cast themselves down into their own light, which is like that of lighted coals, and in some cases like that from burning coals'.

In some respects, Swedenborg's conception of Hell agrees precisely with that in the *Tibetan Book of the Dead.* He says, for example, that 'if a man is in evil, he is tied to Hell, and in respect to his spirit is actually there, and after death desires nothing so much as to be where his evil is. Consequently, it is man who casts himself into Hell after death'. In the *Tibetan Book of the Dead* we are told that the wanderer in the *Bardo* will see a dull, smoke-coloured light and that he will find it pleasant, and will wish to move towards it. There are other similarities as well. Swedenborg also agrees on several points of Plutarch's description, for in one passage he says that 'those who enter from a burning love of evil appear to be cast headlong, with the head downwards and the feet upwards'. This description is also mentioned by Plutarch in *De Sera Numina Vindiciti,* but Swedenborg said that he saw this done to 'one of the most deceitful' of those who 'have been inwardly wicked while maintaining an outward appearance of goodness'.

If Swedenborg's descriptions resemble the visions described by Plutarch as well as the Buddhist conceptions in the *Tibetan Book of the Dead* we would expect to find similarities also between the Buddhist conceptions and Plutarch's visions ... and we do. The similarities here are more striking, though, and there is a different focus. Whereas Swedenborg's Hell is merely depressing,

Plutarch's Hell is genuinely terrifying ... and so is the Hell of the Buddhists. Trungpa says of the Buddhist Hell-dweller that 'he finds himself walking through gigantic fields of red-hot iron, or being chained and marked with black lines and cut apart, or roasting in hot iron crucibles, or boiling in large cauldrons. There is a feeling of being trapped in a small space with no air to breathe and no room in which to move about. Trapped as he is, the Hell-dweller not only tries to destroy the walls of his claustrophobic prison; he even attempts to kill himself'. He cannot die, of course ... he has already done that. The more he struggles, 'the more solid and oppressive the walls of his prison become ... it is by withdrawing from them that they are mastered, for then they disappear'.

Another description of Hell

A Christian churchman whose heart stopped on the operating table for 12 minutes said he was given a tour of Hell and won a reprieve from death so that he could warn mankind of the dangers involved. Doctors in Bern, Switzerland said that Rev. Hans Gerber, a 49-year-old minister, had given a detailed account of his near-death experience and the infamous souls he found in Hell.

'Hell is not an inferno, but quite the opposite', Rev. Gerber said. 'It is an endless frozen expanse where the damned are relentlessly pursued by their victims through eternity'. The minister told a research team investigating the out-of-body experience that he recalls hovering above the operating table while he watched a team of doctors frantically working to save him after his heart stopped during by-pass surgery. 'He watched the scene in the operating room for several moments and then felt himself being drawn into a dark tunnel', said Dr Dieter Oermann, a surgeon in charge of the case. 'Rev. Gerber found himself standing on the ice at the edge of a frozen lake where he saw Adolf Hitler turning blue from the bitter cold and fleeing from an angry mob', said Dr Oermann.

The doctor said that Rev. Gerber witnessed a ghastly scene in which Lee Harvey Oswald was brutally tortured and said he saw Joseph Stalin, Billy the Kid, Attila the Hun and Errol Flynn. 'Even though this was frightening, Rev. Gerber reported that he did not feel that he was in any danger', said Dr Oermann. Doctors were skeptical of Rev. Gerber's story when he woke in the recovery room after his surgery. 'Members of the surgical team requested that Rev. Gerber be placed under hypnosis by a psychologist because they were concerned with his emotional state', said Dr Oermann. 'The more that I, and the psychologists, worked with Rev. Gerber, the more we became convinced he certainly did have an out-of-body experience because he was able to accurately describe activities and events that occurred while he was not only unconscious but clinically dead'.

CHAPTER 14

Here today, back tomorrow

Life beyond life

Many primitive tribes and lost civilizations acknowledged the existence of a life between life; an existence where the soul dwells for a time before returning to spend another lifetime on Earth. It is probable that this is the existence experienced by people who have had an NDE.

Dr Joel Whitton's investigation of the afterlife is one of the most comprehensive ever written. In his book, *Life Between Life* (with Joe Fisher, Time Warner), Dr Whitton, through many hours of hypnotic sleuthing, compiled a collection of personal inventories of past lives extending back hundreds of years. He discovered that, according to karmic necessity, his subjects jumped in and out of incarnation to interact with the same entities in ever-changing relationships. After hundreds of hours of hypnotic sessions, Dr Whitton was obliged to agree with the ancient scriptures which decreed that, in the vast majority of cases, enlightenment is a prize to be won only after a painfully slow journey of purification from body to body. The ancient Egyptians believed that it could take up to 3000 years for an individual to go through his entire cycle of lives.

Plato, in the tenth book of the *Republic*, recounts the story of Er, the Pamphylian, who came back to life on a funeral pyre twelve days after being killed in battle. Er's remarkable story is the oldest personal NDE available and it is reproduced in its entirety in the end pages of this book. In his account, Er spoke graphically of the life between lives, telling how each soul was given the opportunity of selecting the form of its next incarnation. Once this selection was made, the souls drank from the River of Forgetfulness to erase all conscious memory before re-entering a physical body. Such enforced oblivion before rebirth is a persistent theme in religious traditions ranging from Chinese Buddhism to esoteric Christianity. According to the Hebrew Kabbalists the night angel Layela invokes amnesia by giving the hovering soul a little pinch on the nose while applying light pressure to the upper lip. So it is said that we all bear the mark of the angel's finger on our lips.

Reincarnation is the belief that our soul or awareness survives bodily death and returns at varying intervals to be born again into another physical body for the purpose of growing in knowledge, wisdom and self-awareness. In Eastern thought, reincarnation becomes the obvious explanation for the inequities we see in the world around us. Is it fair for an innocent baby to be born into poverty? It is if that poverty is retributive punishment for that soul's greedy action in a previous life. Is it fair for a seemingly good man to suffer the horrors of cancer? It is if he abused his wife and children in a previous life. Is it fair for a bad man to prosper? It is if we know that karmic law is giving him what he deserves. Is it fair for a tyrant to live into his nineties? It is, if we know that in his next life he will suffer for his tyranny. Reincarnation provides an answer to the tough question of world's inequitable treatment of individuals. As more and more people become intrigued with the magnificent possibility of reincarnation, the question is frequently asked if one can believe this concept ... and the answer is yes ... if we believe the evidence. The following stories are representative of many examples and provide substantiation that the theory of reincarnation is best not passed over in silence.

Mummified corpse confirms life beyond death

In the late 1980s archeologists discovered what may be the most conclusive proof of life after death ever ... the corpse of an Indian soldier who had died 133 years before and was living again, reincarnated as a 9-year-old boy. The scientists, a team of four from Palacky University in Czechoslovakia, reportedly followed the instructions of little Charan Varma of Lucknow, India, to find the corpse in a shallow grave. The child insisted that the body was his and studies of the corpse appear to confirm his claims, according to the *New Delhi Press Syndicate*.

'The child says that he was killed by British soldiers while fighting in the Sepoy Rebellion in 1857', a *Syndicate* news reporter wrote. 'He told scientists he was shot twice in the chest, bayoneted repeatedly and slashed with sabres by British troops.

'Examination of the mummified corpse confirms that the body received extensive and fatal wounds that would support the boy's claims. The body is of a man in his 20s who died in the 1850s. The skeleton showed scars on the ribs, consistent with deep stab wounds, markings on the legs and arms consistent with sabre wounds and the fragments of two bullets in the chest cavity.

'Scrapes of cloth and a tarnished brass belt plate in the grave match the descriptions of the uniforms of Indian soldiers in the 1850s'.

The Palacky University archeological team was involved in a dig of prehistoric Indian home sites near Lucknow when news of the small boy's remarkable claims reached them. Charan said that he had lived as Mahdu Pylee in his previous life. Pylee was a native soldier ... or sepoy ... who died during the Indian Mutiny at the age of 27. He had been buried in an unmarked grave near the village of Sitapur, India. 'We interviewed the child and we were deeply impressed', said Dr Karol Tyl, a member of the scientific team. 'The boy offered to lead us the place where Pylee was buried, a place more than 60 miles from his home. He took us there to an abandoned farm near Sitapur and pointed out a spot near a ruined house where a small mound was visible. When we dug into the mound we found the remains of a man who had been buried there for a century and a half'.

Indian newspaper coverage of Charan Varma's reincarnation story has been extensive and details of the archeologist's finds were published in 1990. 'This is the first conclusive evidence ever found that reincarnation is real, not imaginary', Dr Tyl said. 'We want to make sure that our work remains above reproach. We published the results of our finds at the Pylee gravesite in our professional journal. We have no doubt that what we've uncovered is the most important proof ever found that people can die and live again'.

Evidence of reincarnation

In a revealing case of reincarnation, 6-year-old Toran Singh revealed accurate details of his past life ... he even correctly identified his former wife and children and described how he was shot to death, says a university professor. What's more, Toran ... who said he used to be a man named Suresh Verma ... also has a birthmark on his head exactly where Suresh was shot. And Suresh's widow is convinced Toran really was her husband.

'This is a very strong case for reincarnation', said Dr Narender Chadha, a University of Delhi psychology professor who investigated the case that began to unfold in Badh, India, when Toran was 3. The boy was born in December 1983 ... four months after Suresh's death ... to a poor family who had never before heard of Suresh. 'As soon as he was able to talk, Toran told his parents, 'I am Suresh Verma. I have a radio shop in Agra. My wife's name is Uma and we have two sons,' revealed Dr Chadha.

Toran also told his parents that Suresh died after he was attacked and shot in the head. The boy kept insisting that he had another family, so Toran's brother finally travelled eight miles to Agra to check out the story. He was shocked to find that everything Toran had said was true. When Toran's brother told the story to Suresh's widow Uma, she met with the child and his parents the next day, then brought them to Agra to test Toran.

'He knew what kind of car Suresh had', said Uma. 'He also claimed that he had two children, Ronu and Sonu, and those are the names of my children. He asked me if I recalled an outing to a fair in a neighbouring city and I remember it vividly'.

Uma got more spine-tingling surprises when Toran picked Suresh's children out of a crowd of youngsters, identified Suresh in photos and walked into the dead man's shop like he owned it, she said. 'He strode in, slapped a stool ... a habit Suresh had ... then pointed to a showcase and asked, 'When was that built?' The showcase had, in fact, been put up after Suresh's death.

When Dr Chadha conducted his investigation, he found even more uncanny coincidences. 'The autopsy report indicated where the bullet went into Suresh's head ... and that corresponds to a birthmark Toran has on his head', said the professor. 'And there was another wound on Suresh where the bullet came out of his head ... and that corresponds to a smaller birthmark on the child's head. Because of the evidence, this is a very strong case for reincarnation.' Added Suresh's widow; 'I believe Toran is my dead husband. There's no other way he could possibly know the things he knows about my life with Suresh!'

Child geniuses' talent comes from past lives

Catherine Frazier-Dean wrote that a baby spoke within hours of his birth and at 2 could recite biblical history ... a Mexican 2-year-old could handle obscure calculations at lightning speed ... the blind 6-year-old son of a slave played the piano brilliantly the first time he touched one. These are all cases of child prodigies ... and along with other geniuses they're 'strong evidence for reincarnation', declares author and researcher Joe Fisher. 'They show talent and gifts they had acquired in a previous life. Prodigies had no other way of acquiring these skills', said Fisher. Renowned reincarnation expert Brad Steiger added: 'These children inherited their talent from previous lifetimes'.

The baby who spoke within hours of his birth was Christian Friedrich Heinechen who was born in 1721 in Germany. 'At the age of 1, he knew the main events in the first five books of the Old Testament', said Fisher. 'At 2, he knew all of biblical history. At 3, he understood the outlines of world history and geography and spoke Latin and French'.

Incredibly, at age 4 he predicted his own death before year's end. He was right.

The Mexican child genius was Miguel Mantilla. 'People would ask him questions about the day a certain date would fall on and he would answer with tremendous accuracy at lightening speed', said Fisher, who uncovered these amazing prodigies while researching his book, *The Case For Reincarnation*. The piano-playing prodigy was Blind Tom Wiggins, who was born to a slave in Alabama in 1849. His musical genius was discovered when the family who owned his mother heard someone playing their piano at night. It was Tom, who'd crawled in through a window. 'Tom went on to give concerts around the world', said Fisher.

Love at first sight ... the answer?

Love at first sight ... the sudden spark that ignites between a man and a woman who've never met before ... happens because the couple has known each other in a previous life, parapsychology experts claim. 'I have regressed about 800 people, making them recall past lives', said Ian Currie, a parapsychology researcher and lecturer. 'I find that it's very typical of people who have a strong, intimate relationship in the present life to have been connected in a past life'. Noted parapsychology researcher and author Brad Steiger agreed: 'I have been doing past life research for many years and found ample evidence that love at first sight is due to a couple having known each other in one or several past lives. And through reincarnation they have been brought together again and instantly recognized the strong attraction they previously held for each other'.

Steiger recalled one case of a man who fell in love at first sight with a woman. They married ... but he found that he had trouble relating to his children. 'When I regressed this man, I found out that he had been married to his current spouse in another time, during a famine in Ireland, and had buried his children one by one as they starved to death. To protect himself in this lifetime, he was rejecting any emotional attachment to his kids for fear they would die'.

Helen Wambach, author and researcher, told of another couple who had fallen in love at first sight. 'When I regressed the woman, she came up with five past lives with her current spouse, going all the way back before the commencement of the Christian era. People who feel an instant rapport often report having past lives with each other. And these love at first sight encounters are experiences that are much more deeply felt than the common physical attraction one may feel for a person of the opposite sex'.

Reincarnation verses removed from Christian texts

The doctrine of reincarnation is now in conflict with Christianity because the concept was removed from early church texts. Early church fathers accepted the concept of reincarnation and recorded their personal thoughts on the subject. St Jerome, for example, left extensive passages recording his beliefs, saying:

> 'As to the origin of the soul, I remember the question of the whole kuriakos (church); whether it be fallen from heaven, as Pythagoras and the Platonists and Origen believe; or it be of the proper substance of God; or whether they are kept in a repository formerly built by God; or whether they are made by God and sent back into bodies according to that which is written in the Gospel.'

But it is not 'written in the Gospel' or Gospels today.

In several verses of his work called *Confessions* (c. 401), Bishop Augustine personally wrestled with his expression of the 'unexplainable' concept of pre-existence. As the records of St Jerome make clear, the concept of reincarnation was originally included in early Christian Gospels but was censored at a special church council meeting in 553. A notorious prostitute was responsible for those far-reaching changes and her name was Theodore, wife of Roman Emperor Justinian. She severally criticized the Gospel reference to souls being 'sent back into bodies' (Jerome) since those words essentially taught that all humans are equal. That created difficulties for the ruling class who wanted to convince the common people that the nobility were of a higher standing in the community.

Emperor Justinian over-rode any authority that Pope Vigilius may have had and convened a special church council chaired by the Emperor himself. It became known as the Fifth Ecumenical Council of 553, that was, in fact, the second of four church councils held in Constantinople, the next being in 680 and the last in 869 (*Ecclesiastical History*, Du Pin, Vol. I, Dublin, 1783). The first council of Constantinople was that of 381, when Papa Damasus officially banned the Bible and introduced 'curses' into Christian tradition. The express purpose of the meeting was to bribe a majority vote from churchmen in attendance to approve new anathemas (curses) he issued against Gospel doctrine of pre-existence of the soul. The matter is of considerable importance from the purely historical standpoint, and therefore it is desirable to publish the very words of the Decree by which the early church made the doctrine anathema by denouncing it and removing from its theology. This datum of Christian history is an item quite obscure and difficult to locate, therefore its inclusion here should be appreciated by many people. The Decree was couched in the following sentence:

> 'Whosoever shall support the mythical doctrine of the pre-existence of the human soul, and the consequent monstrous opinion of its return to earth, let him be anathema (cursed).'
> (Decree of the Second Council of Constantinople; 553; *Index Expurgatorius Vaticanus*, An exact reprint, Edited by R Gibbings, BA, Dublin, 1837)

An additional three similar anathemas were published as part of the proceedings of the same Council and all aimed at pre-existence, but included references to reincarnation. The occasion and timing of the Decrees are evidence that indicated that the belief in reincarnation was deeply ingrained in general Christian doctrinism.

Although an angry Pope Vigilius was in Constantinople at the time, he refused to attend the Council. There had been intense conflict between Emperor Justinian and Pope Vigilius since 543, when Justinian, at a local synod, condemned the reincarnation teachings of Origen. 'At the instigation of Vigilius, the Council Decrees were contested in some churches and a fearful schism arose that lasted seventy years' (*Encyclopedia Britannica*, 9th Ed., Vol. 10, Pg. 783 onwards).

The sensitive narratives were subsequently removed from Gospels produced from that time onwards and the church today preaches resurrection, not reincarnation.

CHAPTER 15

The trip to the 'other side'

The earliest known description of the journey to the afterlife is found in a remarkable old writing first carved into stone at the dawn of civilization on Earth. That literature is the oldest known to mankind and is erroneously called *The Egyptian Book of the Dead.* The opening passage said this about itself; 'This is a book of exceedingly great secrecy. Let not the eye of any profane behold it ... That would be an abomination. Conceal its existence. *The Book of the Master of the Hidden Places* is its name'. Some call it the Bible of Ancient Egypt but it is much more than that, and in this study, some references are drawn from *The Book of the Master of the Hidden Places.* However, it shall be called by its now commonly known name, the *Book of the Dead,* so as not to cause confusion.

The *Book of the Dead* is the title generally given to the texts because they were found inscribed on the internal walls of tombs or on papyri rolls resting on or near mummies, and because they were deposited with the dead, that title developed in the late 19th Century. The longest papyrus version discovered to date measures

135 feet (41 metres) and 28 inches high (48 cms) and on many occasions, special papyrus rolls were sealed in a hollow statuette shaped like the deceased's favourite god and placed with the mummy.

Over the last 150 years or so, the discovery of burial chambers holding 'funerary texts' revealed to the modern world the innermost sacred secrets of a select body of ancient Egyptian priests. In those times, the *Book of the Dead* revealed the ultimate secrets of the gods and was carefully hidden beyond the eye of the living for what the priests thought would be forever. They believed that secrets revealed in their sacred writing were visible only to the eyes of the soul of the person buried in that crypt and thus preserved from the eyes of the profane.

Some verses of the *Book of the Dead* were later found in the Pyramid Texts which appeared carved in hieroglyphic form on the inside walls of the burial chamber and anteroom of the pyramid of King Unas, last ruler of the Fifth Dynasty (c. 2345 BC). Some of the 189 chapters are so old they were recorded on the sarcophagus of Queen Khnemnefert, who lived around 2700 BC, according to Egyptologist's reckonings. Other hieroglyphs state that one particular chapter of the *Book of the Dead* was in existence during the reign of Hesep-ti, about 4266 BC and was established by Egyptologists as the most ancient documentation of any kind known in the world today.

The most moderate estimate makes certain sections of the *Book of the Dead* more than 6000 years old and archaeological evidence showed that, according to biblical chronology, those writings were in existence before God created the earth. In any case, Egyptologists were justified in estimating the earliest form of the work to be contemporaneous with the foundation of the civilization that came into Egypt thousands of years ago.

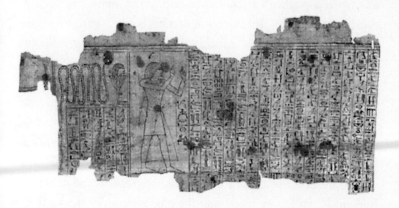

Section of the Egyptian Book of the Dead (Papyrus of RA, c. 1300 BC). The owner of this writing was a wealthy scribe and so able to purchase this expensive, richly illustrated papyrus. To the left is a large figure of RA with his hands raised in prayer.

That fascinating, but perplexing, old writing provides an extensive description of systems of various chambers, passageways, halls, temples and gates that were accessed in a complex journey through twelve divisions of an underworld realm of darkness called *duat*. It also records a compilation of prayers, magic spells and incantations, and lists amulets that were to be worn to provide assistance in safely completing the journey. Although used for funerary purposes, some descriptions provided in the *Book of the Dead* are unconnected with the mystical realm and seem to have originally had an entirely different use. In many cases, explanations are far removed from actual meanings of the passage and are presented in a romanticized manner. It is not an easy book to read but sometimes comments on particular heavenly passages show an accurate grasp of a subject matter having an earthly parallel. For example, seven halls are painstakingly described, along with a detailed description of twenty-one vertical columns or pylons. That documentation is significant for those descriptions are directly associated with the Great Pyramid and the Sphinx at the Giza complex.

The elaborate commentary provided in the *Book of the Dead* seems to have been the work of an intensely formal mind, one that devised a number of explanations that fitted a dual purpose. In simple terms, it was written specifically to be comprehended on two different levels of understanding; esoteric and exoteric. Ancient Egyptians believed that the employment of the texts by the soul of the deceased would give them various divine powers that enabled them to secure acquittal at the Judgment. The numerous pictures and symbols were understood to assist the departed overcome the perils that they believed beset the path of the dead. However, those instructions were also used on the physical Earthly plane by the living and were coded initiatory processes used by ancient Egyptian priesthoods, the original guardians of the Secret knowledge. In other words, the deceased persons in the *Book of the Dead* became the living initiates in Egyptian temples. (The secret initiations are fully described in the author's book, *The Secret in the Bible*).

The *Book of the Dead* is a secret manual of initiation from the mysterious First Times and describes a series of procedures and passwords to be spoken that purposely have two distinct levels of meaning, one spiritual and the other physical. The 'Hidden Places' mentioned in the original title are particular underground chambers at the Giza complex and are described allegorically as mystical places in the abode in heaven. Underlying descriptions given in the *Book of the Dead* are the outlines of an original priestly ritual used in Egyptian temples aeons ago. That ritual was romanticized by the author (authors, maybe) into a supernatural experience disguised as the pathway to be used by the deceased on the journey to the afterlife. In other words, it was possible to duplicate the trip to the heavenly existence while here on Earth. The purpose being to prove to the living that there was an afterlife that could be glimpsed, or experienced, while living the physical life. Therefore, the *Book of the Dead* records the earthly method used in discovering heavenly mysteries of the hereafter, concealed in words and symbols that themselves were hidden in tombs of the deceased.

The *Book of the Dead* carries some unusual narratives, with a curious reference to 'those who live among the stars'. Another passage spoke of a specific knowledge that enabled those in its possession to 'reach the vault of the sky'. The whole of Egyptian theology is clothed in mysterious statements and its arcane writings and secrets in architecture were originally and purposely intended for a great and noble purpose.

CHAPTER 16

Ancient near-death Experiences

Extraordinary as the stories in these pages are, they are by no means unusual. Similar stories have been known and collected since ancient times.

The Adventures of Er, the Pamphylian

This is the oldest known personal record of an NDE and is recorded in the *Republic* of Plato (427-347).

'Well, I said I will tell you a tale; not one of the tales which Odysseus tells to the hero Alcinous, yet this, too, is the tale of a hero, Er, the son of Armenius, a Pamphylian by birth. He was slain in battle, and ten days afterward, when the bodies of the dead were taken up already in a state of corruption, his body was found unaffected by decay, and carried away home to be buried. And on the twelfth day, as he was lying on the funeral pyre, he returned to life and told them what he had seen in the other world.

'He said that when his soul left his body he went on a journey with a great company, and they came to a mysterious place at which there were two openings in the Earth. They were near together, and over against them were two other openings in the heaven above. In the intermediate space there were judges seated, who commanded the just, after they had given judgment on them and had bound their sentences in front of them, to ascend by the heavenly way on the right hand. And in a like manner the unjust were bidden by them to descend by the lower way on the left hand. These also bore the symbols of their deeds, but fastened on their backs. He drew near and they told him that he was to be the messenger who would carry the report of the Other World to men, and they bade him hear and see all that was to be heard and seen in that place. Then he beheld and saw on one side the souls departing at either opening of heaven and earth when sentence had been given on them. And at the two other openings other souls, some ascending out of the Earth dusty and worn with travel, some descending out of heaven clean and bright. And arriving ever and anon they seemed to have come from a long journey, and they went forth with gladness into the meadow, where they encamped as at a festival. And those that knew one another embraced and conversed, the souls which came to Earth curiously enquiring about the things above, and the souls which came from heaven about the things beneath. And they told one another of what happened by the way, those from below weeping and sorrowing at the remembrance of the things that they had endured and seen in their journey beneath the Earth (which journey lasted a thousand years), while those from above were describing heavenly delights and visions of inconceivable beauty.

The story, Glaucon, would take too long to tell, but the sum was this: he said that for every wrong which they had done to anyone they suffered tenfold, or once in a hundred years ... such being reckoned to be the length of a man's life, and the penalty being thus paid ten times in a thousand years. If, for example, there had been any who had been the cause of many deaths, or had betrayed or enslaved cities or armies, or been guilty of any other evil behaviour, for each and all of their offences they received punishment ten times over, and the rewards of beneficence and justice and holiness were in the same proportion. I need hardly repeat what he said concerning young children dying almost as soon as they were born. Of piety and impiety to gods and parents, and of murderers, there were other retributions far greater, which he described. He mentioned that he was present when one of the spirits asked another, 'Where is Aridaeus the Great?'

'Now this Aridaeus lived a thousand years before the time of Er. He had been the tyrant of some in the city of Pamphylia, and had murdered his aged father and his elder brother, and was said to have committed many other abominable crimes. The answer of the other spirit was: ' He comes not hither and will never come'. And this, said he, 'was one of the dreadful sights which we ourselves witnessed. We were at the mouth of the cavern, and having completed all our experiences, were about to reascend, when all of a sudden Aridaeus appeared and several others, most of whom were tyrants. And there were also besides the tyrants more individuals who had been great criminals. They were just, as they fancied, about to return into the upper world, but the mouth, instead of admitting them, gave a roar, whenever any of these incurable sinners, or someone who had not been sufficiently punished, tried to ascend. And these wild men of fiery aspect, who were standing by and heard the sound, seized them and carried them off. And Aridaeus and others they bound foot and hand, and threw them down and flayed them with scourges, and dragged them along the road at the side, carding them on thorns like wool, and declaring to the passers-by what were their crimes, and that they were being taken away to be cast into Hell. And of all the many terrors which they had endured, he said that there was none like the terror which each of them felt at that moment, lest they should hear the voice. And then there was silence, one by one they ascended with exceeding joy. 'These', said Er, 'were the penalties and retributions, and there were blessings as great'.

'Now when the spirits which were in the meadow had tarried seven days, on the eighth they were obliged to proceed on their journey, and, on the fourth day after, he said that they came to a place where they could see from above a line of light, straight as a column, extending right through the whole Heaven and through the Earth, in colour resembling the rainbow, only brighter and purer. Another day's journey brought them to the place, and there in the midst of the light, they saw the ends of the chains of Heaven let down from above. For this light is the belt of Heaven, and holds together the circle of the universe, like the under-girders of a trireme. From this end is extended the spindle of Necessity, on which all the revolutions turn.

'When Er and the other spirits arrived, their duty was to go at once to Lachesis (one of the three Fates, who, according to Plato, sings of the past). But first of all there came a prophet who arranged them in order. Then he took from the knees of Lachesis lives and samples of lives, and having mounted on a high pulpit, spoke as follows, 'Hear the words of Lachesis, the daughter of Necessity. Mortal souls, behold a new cycle of life and mortality.

Your genius will not be allotted to you, but you will choose your genius, and let him who draws the first lot have the first choice, and the life that he chooses shall be his destiny. Virtue is free, and as a man honours and dishonours her he will have more or less of her. The responsibility is with the chooser ... God is justified.

'When the Interpreter had thus spoken he scattered lots indifferently among them all, and each of them took up the lot which fell near him, all but Er himself (he was not allowed). Each as he took his lot perceived the number which he had obtained. Then the Interpreter placed on the ground before them the samples of lives, and there were many more lives than there were souls present, and they were all sorts. There were lives of every animal and of man in every condition. And there were tyrannies among them, some lasting out the tyrant's life, others which broke in the middle and came to an end in poverty and exile and beggary. And there were lives of famous men, some who were famous for their form and beauty as well as for their strength and success in games, or again, for their birth, and the qualities of their ancestors, and some who were the reverse of famous for the opposite qualities. And of women likewise. There was not, however, any definite character in them, because the soul, when choosing a new life, must of necessity become different. But there was every other quality, and they all mingled with one another, and also with elements of wealth and poverty, and disease and health.

'And there were mean states also. And according to the messenger from the other world, this is what the prophet said at the time. 'Even for the last comer, if he chooses wisely and will live diligently, there is appointed a happy and not an undesirable existence. Let not him who chooses first be careless, and let not the last despair'. When he had spoken, who had the first choice came forward, and in a moment chose the greatest tyranny. His mind having been darkened by folly and sensuality, he had not thought the whole matter out before he chose, and did not at first sight perceive that he was fated, among other evils, to devour his own children. But when he had time to reflect, and saw what was in his lot, he began to beat his breast and lament over his choice, forgetting the proclamation of the prophet. For instead of throwing the blame of his misfortune on himself, he accused chance and the gods and everything rather than himself. Now he was one of those who came from heaven, and in a former life had dwelt in a well-ordered State. But his virtue was a matter of habit only, and he had no philosophy. Of others who were similarly overtaken, the greater number came from heaven and therefore had never been schooled by trial, whereas the pilgrims who came from Earth, having themselves suffered and seen others suffer, were not in a hurry to choose. And owing to this inexperience of theirs, and also because the lot was a chance, many of the souls exchanged a good destiny for an evil one, or an evil destiny for a good one. For if a man had always on his arrival in this world dedicated himself from the first to sound philosophy, and had been moderately fortunate in the number of the lot, he might, as the messenger reported, be happy here, and also his journey to another life would be smooth and heavenly, instead of being rough and underground.

'The spectacle was most curious', said he, 'for the choice of the souls was in most cases based on their experience of a previous life'. About the middle came the lot of Atlanta. She, seeing the great fame of an athlete, was unable to resist the temptation.

And after her followed the soul of Epeus the son of Panopeus passing into the nature of a woman cunning in the arts. There came also the soul of Odysseus, having yet to make a choice, and his lot happened to be the last of them all. The recollection of former toils had disenchanted him of ambition, and he went about for a considerable time in search of the life of a private man who had no cares. He had some difficulty in finding this, which was lying about and had been neglected by everybody else. And when he saw it, he said that he would have done the same had his lot been first instead of last, and that he was delighted to have it.

'All the souls had now chosen their lives, and they went in order of their choice to Lachesis, who sent with them the genius which they had severally chosen, to be the guardian of their lives and the fulfiller of the choice. This genius led the soul to Clotho, and drew them within the revolution of the spindle impelled by her hand, thus ratifying the destiny of each, and then, when they were fastened to this, to Atropos, who spun the threads and made them irreversible, whence without turning they passed beneath the Throne of Necessity. And when they had all passed, they marched on in a scorching heat to the plane of Forgetfulness, which was a barren waste, destitute of trees and verdure, and then towards evening they camped by the river of Unmindfulness, whose waters no vessel may hold. Of this they were all obliged to drink a certain quantity, and those who were not saved by wisdom drank more than was necessary. And as each one drank he forgot all things.

'After they had gone to rest, about the middle of the night, there was a thunderstorm and an earthquake, and they were driven upwards in all manners of ways to their birth, like stars shooting through the sky. Er himself was hindered from drinking the water. But in what manner or by what means he returned, he could not say. Only, in the morning, awakened suddenly, he found himself lying on a funeral pyre'.

The Experience of Timarchus in the Other World

The following NDE is found in Plutarch's (46-120) essay called 'A Discourse Concerning Socrates' Daemon' and is nearly two thousand years old.

'Timarchus, fell down and struck his head and through the parted sutures of his skull his soul flew out, which now being loose and mixed with a purer and lighter air, was most jocund and well pleased. It seemed to begin to breathe as if formerly it had been choking, and it grew in size, like a sail swollen by the wind. Then he heard a small noise whirling about his head, very sweet and ravishing. Looking up he saw no Earth, but instead saw innumerable islands, unequal in size, but completely surrounding him, shining with a gentle fire, and changing colours with the variation in the light. The whirling of the islands, it is likely, agitated the ether, and made the sound, for the ravishing softness of it was very agreeable to their even motions.

'Between these islands was a large sea or lake, which shone very gloriously, being adorned with a gay variety of colours mixed with blue. Some few of the islands swam in the sea, and were carried to the other side of the current. Others, as these were the most, were carried up and down, tossed, whirled, and almost overwhelmed. The sea in some places seemed very deep, especially towards the south, and in others very shallow. It ebbed and flowed, but the tides were neither high nor strong. In some parts its colour was pure and sea-green. In others it looked troubled and muddy as a pool. The current brings those islands that were carried over to the other side back again, but not to the same point, so that their motions are not exactly circular but winding. About the middle of these islands, the ambient sea seemed to bend into a hollow, a little less, it appeared to him, than eight parts of the whole. Into this sea were two entrances, by which it received two opposite fiery rivers, running in with so strong a current that it spread a fiery white over a great part of the blue sea.

'The sight pleased him very much, but when he looked downward, there appeared a vast chasm. It was round, as if he had looked into a divided sphere, very deep and frightful, full of thick darkness, which was every now and then troubled and disturbed. Thence a thousand howlings and bellowings of beasts, cries of children, moans of men and women, and all sorts of terrible noises reached his ears, but faintly, as being far off and rising through the vast hollow, and this terrified him exceedingly. A little while after, an invisible Being spoke to him: 'Timarchus, what do you wish to understand?' And he replied: 'Everything, for what is there here that is not wonderful and surprising?

'We have little to do with those things above', said the Being, 'for they belong to other gods, but as for Proserpina's quarter ... which is one of the four quarters, as the River Styx divides them ... that we govern, and you may visit if you wish'.

'But what is Styx?'

'The way to hell, which reaches to the contrary quarter, and with its head divides the light. For, as you see, it rises from hell below, and as it rolls on touches also the light, and is the extreme limit of the Universe. There are four divisions of all things. The first is of life, the second of motion, the third of generation and the fourth of corruption. The first is coupled to the second by a unit, invisible in substance. The second is coupled to the third by understanding, in the Sun, and the third to the fourth by Nature, in the Moon. Over each of these ties a Fate presides. Over the first, Atropos, over the second, Clotho, and over the third, Lachesis, who is the Moon, and about whom is the third whirl of generation. All of the other islands have gods in them; but the Moon, belonging to earthly daemons, is raised but a little above the Styx. Styx seizes upon her once in a hundred and seventy-seven second revolutions, and when it approaches the souls are startled, and cry out for fear; for hell swallows up a great many, and the Moon receives some swimming up from below which have run through their whole course of generation, unless they are wicked and impure. For against such she throws flashes of lightening, makes horrible noises, and frightens them away, so that, missing their desired happiness and bewailing their condition, they are carried down to undergo another generation.

'But' said Timarchus, 'I see nothing but stars leaping about the hollow, some carried into it, and some darting out of it again'.

'These', said the Voice, 'are daemons; for thus it is. Every soul has some portion of reason. A man cannot be a man without it. But as much of each soul as is mixed with flesh and appetite is changed, and through pain or pleasure becomes irrational. Every soul does not mix itself after one sort; for some plunge into the body, and so in this life their whole frame is corrupted by appetite and passion. Others are mixed as to some part, but the purer part still remains without the body. It is not drawn down into it, but swims above, and touches the extremest part of man's head. It is like a *cord* to hold up and direct the subsiding part of the soul, as long as it proves obedient and is not overcome by the appetites of the flesh. That part that is plunged into the body is called the soul, but the uncorrupted part is called the mind, and the vulgar think it is within them, as likewise they imagine the reflected image to be within the glass.

'But the more intelligent, who know it to be without, call it a *daemon*. Therefore, those stars which you see extinguished, imagine to be souls whose whole substances are plunged into bodies. And those that recover their light and rise from below, that shake off the ambient darkness, as if it were dirt and clay, know to be sure to retire from their bodies after death. And those that are carried up on high are the daemons of wise men and philosophers. But pray pry narrowly and endeavour to discover the tie by which everyone is united to a soul.

'Upon this Timarchus looked as steadfastly as he could, and saw some of the stars very much agitated, and some less, as corks upon a net, and some whirled around like a spindle, having a very irregular and uneven motion, not being able to run in a straight line. And to this the Voice said: 'Those that have a straight and regular motion belong to souls which are very manageable, by reason of their genteel breeding and philosophical education, and which upon earth do not plunge themselves into the foul clay and become irrational. But those that move irregularly, sometimes upwards, sometimes downwards, as striving to break loose from a vexing chain, are yoked to and strive with very intractable conditions, which ignorance and want of learning make headstrong and ungovernable.

Sometimes they get the better of the passions, and draw them to the right side. Sometimes they are drawn away by them, and sink into sin and folly, and then again endeavour to get out. For the tie is, as it were, a bridle on the irrational part of the soul, and when it is pulled back, draws in repentance for past sins, and shame for loose and unlawful pleasures, which is a pain and stoke inflicted upon the soul by a governing and prevailing power. By this means it becomes gentle and manageable, and like a tamed beast, without blows or torment, it understands the minutest direction of the daemon. Such indeed are but very slowly and very hardly brought to a right temper, but of that sort which from the very beginning are governable and obedient to the direction of the daemon, and those prophetic souls, those intimates of the gods. Such was the soul of Hermodorus the Clazomenian, of which it is reported that for several days and nights it would leave his body, travel over many counties, and return after it had viewed things and discoursed with persons at a great distance, till at last, by the treachery of his wife, his body was delivered to his enemies, and they burned his house while he was 'out'.

'It is certain that this is mere fable. For the soul never went out of the body, but loosened the tie that held the daemon, and permitted it to wander, so that the daemon, seeing and hearing, brought the news back to the soul. Yet those that burned his body are even to this time severely tormented in the deepest pit of hell. But this, youth, you shall more clearly perceive three months hence; now depart.

'The Voice continuing no longer, Timarchus (as he said) turned around to discover who it was had spoken, but a violent pain seized his head, as if his skull had been pressed together, so that he lost all sense and understanding. But in a little while recovering, he found himself in the entrance of the cave, where he at first fell down'.

The Experiences of Thespesius of Soli in the Other World

As told by Plutarch (46-120) this account provides descriptions of soul colours, mentions the soul being attached to the body by a cord, and includes an intriguing section on souls being prepared for reincarnation.

'There was one Thespesius of Soli, the friend and familiar acquaintance of that Protogenes who for some time conversed among us. This gentleman in his youth led a debauched and intemperate life, in a short time spent his patrimony, and then for some years became very wicked, but afterwards repented of his former follies and extravagances, and pursuing the recovery of his lost estate by all manner of tricks and shifts, did as is usual with dissolute and lascivious youths, who, when they have wives of their own, never mind them at all, but when they have dismissed them, and find them married to others that watch them with a more vigilant affection, endeavour to corrupt and vitiate them by all the unjust and wicked provocations imaginable. In this humour, abstaining from nothing that was lewd and illegal, so it tended to his gain and profit, he got no great manner of wealth, but procured to himself a world of infamy by his unjust and knavish dealing with all sorts of people.

'Yet nothing made him more the talk of the country, than the answer which was brought him back from the oracle of Amphilocus. For thither it seems he sent to inquire of the god whether he should live any better during the remainder of his life, to which the oracle answered, that he would live better after he had died. And not long after the thing came true. For he happened to fall from a certain precipice upon his neck, and though he received no wound nor broke any limb, yet the force of the fall knocked the wind out of him. Three days after, being carried forth to be buried, just as he was about to be let into the grave, suddenly he came to himself, and recovered his strength, and so altered the course of his life, that it was almost incredible to those who knew him. For by the report of the Cilicians, there never was in that age a more just person in common dealings between man and man, or more devout and religious as to divine worship, or more an enemy to the wicked, or more constant and faithful to his friends.

'For that reason, those who knew him well wanted to hear from him the cause of such great alteration, not believing that such a thing could come about by mere chance, though it seems as if it did just that, as he related to Protogenes and others of his closest friends.

'For when his sense left his body, he felt as he would if he had been a pilot flung from the helm of his ship and into the sea by the force of a storm. Afterwards, rising up above the water by degrees, so soon as he thought he had fully recovered his breath, he looked about him every way, as if one eye of his soul had been opened. But he beheld none of the things which he formerly had been wont to see.

'Instead he saw stars of vast magnitude, at immense distances from one another, and sending forth a light so wonderful for the brightness of its colour, which shot itself out in length with incredible force, on which the soul, riding as it were in a chariot, was most swiftly, yet as gently and smoothly, dangled from one place to another. But omitting the greatest part of the sights that he beheld, he saw, as he said, the souls of such as were newly dead, as they mounted from below, resembling little fiery bubbles, to which the air gave way. These bubbles afterwards broke insensibly and by degrees, the soul coming forth from them in the shapes of men and women, light and nimble, as being discharged of all earthly substance.

'However, they differed in their motion. For some of them leaped forth with a wonderful swiftness, and mounted up a direct line. Others, like so many spindles of spinning wheels turned round and round, sometimes whirling upwards, sometimes darting downwards, with a confused and mixed agitation, that could hardly be stopped in a very long time.

'He did not know most of these souls, but, perceiving two or three of his acquaintances, he endeavoured to approach and talk to them. But they neither heard him speak, nor, for that matter, did they seem to be in their right mind, fluttering and out of their senses, disdaining either to be seen or felt. They frisked up and down at first, alone and apart by themselves, till meeting at length with others in the same condition, they clung together. But still their motions were with the same giddiness and uncertainty as before, without steerage or purpose. And they made sounds like the cries of soldiers in combat, intermixes with doleful yells of fear and lamentation. Others towered aloft in the upper regions of the air, and these looked gay and pleasant, and frequently accosted each other with kindness and respect. They shunned the troubled souls, and seemed to show discontent by crowding together, and joy and pleasure by expanding and separating from each other.

'One of these said he, being the soul of a certain kinsman whom he did not know well, the person having died when very young, drew near him, and saluted him by the name of Thespesius. At this he was amazed, and said that his name was not Thespesius but Aridaeus, whereupon the spirit replied, 'it was true that you were once called that, but from now on you shall be called Thespesius, which is to say, 'divine'.

'For you are not numbered among the dead yet, but by a certain Destiny and permission of the gods you are come here with only your Mind, having left the rest of your soul, like an anchor, in your body. And that you may be assured of this, observe that the souls of the dead do not cast a shadow or open or shut their eyelids'.

'Thespesius, having heard this, was so much more encouraged to make use of his own reason. And looking around to perceive the truth of what he had been told, he saw there a kind of **obscure and shadowlike line** (reference to a cord) followed him, whereas the other souls shone like a round body of perfect light, and were transparent within.

'And yet there was a very great difference between even those. For some yielded a **smooth**, even and **continuous** lustre, all of one **colour**, like the full moon in her bright splendour, and others were marked with long scales or slender streaks. Still others were covered with black speckles like the skins of vipers, and there were yet others who were marked with faint scratches. (reference to colours of souls)

'At this Thespesius' kinsman told him several things, how Adrastea, daughter of Jupiter and of Necessity, sat in the highest place of all, to punish every sort of crime. And that in the whole number of the wicked and ungodly, there was not one ... great or little, high or low, rich or poor ... who could escape by force or cunning the severe lashes of her rigour. But as there are three sorts of punishments, so there are three Furies, or female ministers of Justice; and to each of these belongs a particular office and degree of punishment. The first of these was called Speedy Punishment (Poine), who takes charge of those who are to receive punishment while still in the body, and who she manages in a gentle manner, ignoring many offences which need expiation. If a greater labour is required, they are delivered to Justice (Dike) and if Dike has given them up as incorrigible, then the third and most severe of all Adrastea's ministers, Erinnys, takes them in hand. And after she has chased them from one place to another, flying, yet not knowing where to go for shelter or relief, plagued and tormented with a thousand miseries, she plunges them headlong into an invisible abyss, the hideousness of which no tongue can express.

'Now of all these three sorts, that which is inflicted by punishment in this life resembles the practice among the barbarians. For as the Persians take off the garments and turbans of those they would punish, and tear and whip the garments before the offender's faces, while the criminals beg for mercy with tears and lamentations, so corporal punishments, mulcts, and fines, have no severity, and do not take hold of the vice itself, but are inflicted mostly with regard to appearances and the senses. But if anyone comes hither who has escaped punishment while he lived upon the earth, and before he was well purged from his crimes, Justice takes him to task, naked, with his soul in full view, and with nothing to conceal his criminality, but on all sides and to all men's eyes exposed, she shows him first to his honest parents, if he had any, that they may see how degenerate he was, and how unworthy of his progenitors. But if his parents were also wicked, then are their sufferings rendered yet more terrible by the mutual sight of each other's miseries, and this continues for a long time, until every crime has been effaced with torments which as much surpass the miseries of the flesh, as these surpass a mere idle dream. But the welts and stripes that remain after punishment appear more obvious in some, less evident in others'.

'See there, he said, **the colours of different souls**. The black and sordid hue is the colour of avarice and fraud. The bloody and flame-like colour betokens cruelty and lust for revenge. Where you see the bluish colour, it is a sign that the soul will hardly be cleansed from the impurities of lascivious pleasure and voluptuousness.

'Finally the dark violet, and venomous colour, which resembles the ink spewed by a cuttle fish, comes from envy. For as during life the wickedness of the soul, being governed by the passions and in turn governing the body, occasions this variety of colours: so here it is the end of expiation and punishment, when these are cleansed away, and the soul recovers her native lustre and becomes clear and spotless. But so long as these remain there, so will certain returns of the passions, accompanied with little pantings and beatings, as if it were of the pulse, in some remiss and languid, and quickly extinguished, and in others more quick and vehement. Some of these souls, being born again and again chastised, recover a due habit and disposition, while others, by the force of ignorance and the enticing show of pleasure, are carried into the bodies of brute beasts. For while some, through the feebleness of their reasoning ability, are compelled by their active principle to seek a new incarnation, others, lacking temperance, wish to gratify their desires. Here (on the astral plane) there is nothing but an imperfect shadow and dream of pleasure which cannot be realized.

'Having said this, the spirit carried Thespesius to a certain place, which it appeared to him there were wide open spaces, yet so gently, that he seemed to be borne on rays of light, as if upon wings. At last he came to a gaping chasm which appeared to be bottomless, and there he found himself deserted by the extraordinary force that brought him there. He saw other souls there in the same condition as myself. They hovered in flocks like birds, flying around and around the mouth of the chasm, but not daring to enter.

'Within, the chasm resembled the groves of Bacchus, fringed about with the pleasing verdure of various herbs and plants, and yielding a delightful prospect of all sorts of flowers, interrupting the greenness with a wonderful variety of colours, and at the same time offering a gentle breeze, which graced the air with perfumes as delightful to the souls as the fragrance of wines is to us on earth. The souls that partook of these fragrances were almost all dissolved in raptures of mirth and caresses. There was nothing to be heard for some distance but laughter, and all the sounds of merriment which are common among those who pass their time in sport.

'The spirit said that Bacchus ascended by this route to heaven, and afterwards returning fetched Semele the same way. It was called the Place of Oblivion (Lethe). He would therefore not suffer Thespesius to tarry there, and carried him away against his will, instructing him by this experience how easy the mind is carried away by pleasure, and that the irrational part, having thus been awakened, revives the memory of the body. From this proceeds desire and an appetite for reincarnation. It occurs when the soul is weighed down with too much moisture.

'After he had been carried the same distance in the other direction, Thespesius thought he saw an enormous goblet, into which several rivers emptied. Among them was one which was whiter than snow. Another resembled a rainbow. The tinctures of the rest were varied. As he drew nearer, the air became more rarefied and the colours disappeared, so that the goblet was perfectly white, and he saw three daemons sitting together in a triangular formation, mixing the rivers together in certain measures. Thus far, said Thespesius' guide, did Orpheus come when he sought for the soul of his wife. When he returned to earth, he remembered what he had seen only imperfectly, and popularized a false conception.

'Orpheus said that the Delphic oracle was common to Night and Apollo, whereas Apollo never had anything to do with Night. But said his spirit, it is common to Night and the Moon, which is not within the earth's boundaries, and has no fixed or certain seat, but wanders among men in dreams and visions. For it is for this reason that dreams are confused, compounded as they are of truth and falsehood intermixed. But concerning the oracle of Apollo, said the spirit, you neither see it, nor can behold it. For the earthbound part of the soul cannot let itself loose, and therefore cannot ascend to sublimity (Devachan), but tends earthward, being fastened to the body.

'With that, leading Thespesius nearer, the spirit endeavoured to show him the light of the Tripod, which, as he said, fell upon Parassus after shooting through the bosom of Themis, Thespesius wanted to see this, but could not, since he was dazzled by the extraordinary brilliance of the light. Passing by, he heard the shrill voice of a woman speaking in verse, and, as he thought, foretelling the time of his own death, among other things. This, the spirit told him, was the voice of a Sybil, who was whirled about in orbit across the face of the Moon, and who continually sang of future events. He wanted to hear more but he was tossed in the opposite direction by the motion of the Moon, as by the force of rolling waves, so that he could hear very little, and that only in bits and pieces. Among other things, the prophecies concerning Mount Vesuvius, and the destruction of Dicaearchia by fire, together with the fragment of a verse concerning an emperor of his time.

'Who, though such just that no man could accuse. However, his empire should by sickness lose.'

'After this, they passed on to see the torments of the damned, and they did indeed see some dismal sights. Thespesius unexpectedly found himself among his friends and relatives, who were groaning and calling him by name. At length he saw his father ascending from a certain abyss, covered with stripes, gashes and scars. He was not permitted to keep silence, but was compelled to make confession by his tormentors, and stretching out his hands, admitted that he had poisoned some of his guests for the sake of their gold. He had gone undetected in life, but was convicted in death, and had already undergone some of his punishments, and was being summoned to a place where he would undergo even more. Thespesius was so frightened by this that he did not dare intercede on his father's behalf. He wanted very much to leave, and looked around for his guide, but he was nowhere to be seen.

'He was pushed forward by deformed and grim-faced goblins, and found that the shadows of those that had been notorious criminals in this life had been punished in life, were not punished so grievously as the others, nor even in the same manner, for their tendency towards vice comes from an imperfection in the irrational part of their soul. As for those who concealed their vice with an outward show of virtue, their tormentors turned them inside out, causing them great pain, like the sea scolopenders, which, having swallowed a hook, threw out their bowels and lick it out again. Others they flayed and terrified, to bring their secret hypocrisies and latent impieties, which possessed and corrupted the principal part of their souls, into the open. Still others he saw, who were intertwined in twos and threes, and who devoured each other, either because of ancient grudges, or else in revenge for injuries suffered while on earth.

'Moreover, he said that there were certain lakes, equidistant one from the other, one of boiling cold, another of frozen lead, and still another of scaly and rugged iron. By the sides of these stood certain daemons with instruments, who lowered and raised the souls of avaricious and greedy men like smiths in a forge. For the flame of the golden furnace having rendered these souls of a fiery and transparent colour, they plunged them into that of lead, where after they were congealed and hardened into a substance like hail, they were thrown into the lake of iron, where they became black and deformed, and being broken and crumbled by the roughness of the iron, changed their form. In all these transformations they endured the most dreadful torments. But they who suffered the most were those that believed that the divine vengeance had no more in store for them, and were seized and dragged to further execution. And these were those for whom their posterity suffered. For when any of the souls of those children meet those of their parents or ancestors, they fly into a rage, and accuse them, and show them the marks of what they have endured. The parents try to hide themselves, but the others follow them, and lay such bitter taunts upon them, that their tormentors lay hold of them and take them to new torments, howling and yelling at the very thought of what they had endured already. He said that as they murmured their complaints, some of these souls of posterity swarmed together like bees or bats.'

'The last thing he saw there were the **souls** of those who were **destined for reincarnation**. They were bowed, bent, and transformed into all sorts of creatures with tools and anvils which certain workmen, appointed for the purpose, used without mercy, bruising the limbs of some, braking those of others, disjointing others, and pounding still others to powder, to render them fit for other lives. Among them he saw the soul of Nero being grievously tortured in many ways, but especially by being transfixed with nails. This soul the workmen took in hand, but when they had forged it into the form of one of Pindar's vipers, which eats its way to life through the bowels of the female, suddenly a conspicuous light shone forth, and a voice was heard out of the light, which ordered the soul transfigured again into some other, more gentle creature, and so they made it resemble one of the creatures that sing and croak at the side of ponds and marshes. For indeed he had been punished in some measure for his crimes, and besides, the gods owed him some compassion. He restored the Greeks to their liberty, and the Greeks were of all his subjects the most beloved of the gods.

'As he was about to return (to his body), a woman, admirable for her form and stature, took him by the arm, saying, 'Come hither, that thou mayest the better be able to retain the remembrance of what thou hast seen'. With that, she was about to strike him with a small fiery wand, similar to the kind painters use, but another woman prevented her. And then he thought himself whirled away by a strong and violent wind and forced as it were through a pipe. And so, lighting again into his own body, he awoke and found himself on the brink of his own grave'. (reference to reincarnation)

CONCLUSION

It is possible to see from these three ancient accounts that the knowledge of a life beyond death is very old indeed.

As happened back in the time of Plato, many people today speak fondly of their beautiful experience, and these reports are too numerous to be discounted as imagination.

In these pages I have tried to present an overview of available evidence of these age-old phenomena that *do* exist and are a marvellous and exciting facet of human life.

Without exaggeration, millions of people have undergone the sorts of experiences that are recorded in this book.

A Gallup Poll conducted in the USA in the mid-eighties concluded that eight million Americans had had a near-death experience. The sheer bulk of information available today makes possible the fact-based and realistic belief that we survive the physical death of our bodies and are renewed in some other guise and existence.

The evidence of a world beyond the grave continues to grow and the only conclusion seems to be that the human personality can and does operate away from the human body and continues to do so after physical death.

Millions of people just like you have said ... *there is life beyond death.*

A NOTE TO READERS

Can you contribute a personal experience?

**Have you ever been on the verge of death or had a close call
which involved any unusual experience?**

I am making an extensive study of all areas related to cases
suggestive of survival after death and would appreciate
hearing in detail about what happened to you. Please write
to me of your experience. (See submission guidelines below.)

Tony Bushby

Send your stories to:

Joshua Books
PO Box 5149
Maroochydore BC
Queensland 4558
Australia

Your submission:

Please send in hardcopy format only. (Do not send by email or disc)
Please keep a copy of your manuscript as submissions will not be returned.
Please advise if Joshua Books has permission to publish your experience.
Joshua Books reserves the right to edit any material used for publication.
Joshua Books takes due care but no responsibility for any material submitted.